FOUR-MINUTE TALKS FOR LAYMEN

Gene E. Bartlett
Roger Fredrikson
Thomas Kilgore, Jr.
Lee Shane

Walter I. Fishbaugh
John P. Gates
Gustav H. Schlauch
Edwin H. Tuller

FOUR-MINUTE TALKS
FOR LAYMEN

The Judson Press
Valley Forge

CONTENTS

FOREWORD

ONE OF THE UNUSUAL MINISTRIES OF THE AMERICAN BAPTIST CONvention is *The Laymen's Hour,* a radio program originated in 1947 and which recognized 20 years of continuous broadcasting in 1967. During the past two decades the program has mellowed and matured, but instead of adopting a position of an "elder statesman" it is still young in concept, active and progressive, winning more friends to its message with each succeeding year.

In fact, at this writing the program is broadcast *on more stations than during any other year in its history . . . and on higher powered stations . . . and in the leading population centers across the nation.*

There must be a reason for this continuous, expansive interest and high degree of acceptance by the stations. And there is. One of its originators, Gilbert B. Brink, is at the helm and produces the program in association with a highly skilled and professionally competent group of workers.

Today, the singers meet on an average of once each month to record the music for four programs. Woven between hymns and anthems are the pre-taped recordings of Art Gilmore's introductions and Scripture readings, and finally there is added the recording of the speaker's message which had been taped months before in some city in the East, Midwest, or on the West Coast.

To bring together all the segments which constitute a program, exact and detailed planning has been carried on for many previous months. It is done by a crew which includes a script writer, music committee, program coordinator, announcer, speaker, producer. (There are still others who are involved after the program has been broadcast, i.e., the retired folk at the Atherton Home who answer the mail; the unheralded dedicated men working in behalf of the American Baptist Men who maintain a rapport with the stations and interest new ones in the program.)

The music of *The Laymen's Hour* is provided by one of the finest men's choruses on the air. They have recorded several albums, and individually and collectively their services are in great demand.

Eight speakers are invited to participate. Four of them prepare 12 four-minute messages; the rest only one each. These messages must be written, edited, and recorded not later than three months preceding the year in which they are to be broadcast! Thus, a speaker preparing a Christmas message must do so a year and a half before it is heard in the homes across the country and around the world.

The speakers are carefully chosen; not everyone has the ability to communicate the gospel cogently and reach an unseen responsive audience — and do it all in four minutes!

To illustrate, here are 52 talks which were broadcast on *The Laymen's Hour*. If proof of their effectiveness were needed, we could produce thousands of requests from listeners for copies of these messages. Why did these talks draw such mail? The answer is deceptively simple; they spoke to the listener in language, thought, and relevance — a contemporary presentation of the gospel — and did it all in *four minutes!*

We trust that you will find these talks helpful not only for your own personal reading but for guidance when you are called to deliver brief inspirational messages in church, civic, school, and other groups. You will find some of them suitable for use in these settings with very little change; others will suggest ideas and illustrations for talks of your own.

And with deep gratitude to our speakers for making this volume possible, we offer it to you.

FREDERICK L. ESSEX, *Director*
Radio-Television Department
Division of Communication
American Baptist Convention

January 3, 1966

Gene E. Bartlett . . . *is president of Colgate Rochester Divinity School. He has held several pastorates, including Calvary Baptist Church in Syracuse, N.Y.; the First Baptist Church in Columbia, Missouri; the First Baptist Church in Evanston, Illinois; and the First Baptist Church in Los Angeles. He is the author of several published articles and two books:* The News in Religion *and* The Audacity of Preaching. *Dr. Bartlett has served his denomination as a member of its Board of Education and Publication, as chairman of its Convention Program Committee, and as a member of its Radio and Television Committee. He has also taken a significant part in various ecumenical activities.*

1. THE EYE OF THE STORM

THERE ARE TIMES OF THE YEAR WHEN STORMS BECOME FRONT PAGE news. Warnings go up in the coastal areas where winds roar in from the sea, leave their devastation, and disappear again. For some reason we have given these storms feminine names! I suspect this custom started when some weatherman drew upon personal experience and saw his chance!

Actually scientists tell us that across the face of the earth an estimated 44,000 storms take place every day — thunderstorms, tornadoes, cyclones, hurricanes. There seems to be, in short, a constant turbulence in the atmosphere.

One of the most devastating disturbances — the kind that sends up the warnings along our coastal areas — is, of course, the hurricane. Its winds have a tremendous velocity and carry everything before them. Yet we are told that there is a strange characteristic of this kind of storm. While the winds move in a great circular sweep, at the center there is almost absolute calm. This is called the eye of the storm. It's said that the winds nearest the center are often the strongest, running from 150 to 250 miles an hour. Yet they swirl around a silent core of calm. Sailors even report experiences of being completely surrounded by the roar of great winds, yet riding on quiet seas. What a strange phenomenon it is — the eye of the storm, the calm at the center!

But it's no more amazing than a spiritual experience which is reported at many points in the Bible. Beyond doubt, God has provided such a center in many of our personal experiences. Among many witnesses to this in the biblical story, the word of the prophet Isaiah seems to state it most simply. Out of his own experience he addressed himself thankfully to God, "Thou dost keep him in perfect peace, whose mind is stayed upon thee."

Perhaps this is the fulfillment of that phrase we often use, "the peace that passes understanding." There is *some* peace which is quite understandable. When all is well and life has struck a harmony, peace is exactly what you would expect. When health is your possession and favor rests upon all your circumstances, it would be strange *not* to have peace. But when that peace comes in the midst of storm, when it is like the calm at the center of a hurricane, that indeed *is* the peace that passes understanding. It isn't at all what you would expect. And when it comes, it always brings a note of surprise. You are grateful for it, deeply grateful, even when you can't explain it.

Dr. James A. Francis was pastor to a great church in the days when a new building was being erected to the glory of God and as a great center of ministry in an expanding city. Those years were most difficult ones, especially since his health was failing. Yet those who really knew him testified that he carried his responsibility with a surprising serenity. He lived to see the dedication of that new sanctuary, but shortly afterward death came. The chapel which bears his name has a bronze marker at the entrance. Some days, when we too were under the stresses of our time, it was an inspiration to stop and read the inscription. The words were chosen especially because those who knew him felt they most fittingly described his life. A close friend wrote of him in those days, "I look at him in the midst of the storms that beat upon him, and I find him as calm and steady as if nothing had happened. When the time came for him to walk down the valley of the shadow of death, he walked straight toward it as if he were going to a crown."

Now that's a remarkable witness to leave. Somehow over the years his witness has been a part of the comfort which he continued to impart to men and women through that church. It confirms the truth of the prophet Isaiah that there is an eye of the storm, and grateful are those who find it. He does keep in perfect peace those whose minds are stayed upon him.

2. WHAT'S THE SENSE IN SUFFERING?

IT ISN'T DIFFICULT TO UNDERSTAND WHAT PROMPTED THE ELDERLY MAN of salty disposition to say one day that the first thing he was going to do in heaven was to get God in a corner and ask him some questions! In the face of some circumstances of life, most of us have known that mood. And one of the first questions we would be tempted to ask is: What's the sense in suffering?

For us the question has to reach out for a Christian answer and thereby we come to one of the most practical points of our faith. For the Christian view of suffering has a realism about it. It has held that, even when we cannot answer *why*, we still must answer *how* — that is, how suffering can be overcome. Maude Royden who distinguished herself as a preacher in England, and who was well acquainted with suffering herself, used to say: "If anyone asks me to explain suffering, I say I can't. I only say I have a power which can surmount it."

This brings to our minds some words ascribed to Joseph in the Book of Genesis. In that story, we are reminded that Joseph was sold by his brothers into Egypt, where he suffered privation and even imprisonment, yet rose to be a ruler close to Pharaoh. When his children were born, Joseph wanted to give them names which would express his thanksgiving to God. So he named one Manasseh, which means "forgetful," because God had helped him to forget his adversities. But he named the second Ephraim, which means "fruitful." And he explained the choice of names in these words: "God had made me fruitful in the land of my affliction." And that is still the Christian hope!

In the time of suffering, faith alone enables us to wait patiently to see what the outcome is to be. Isn't it true that in the deepest things of life this is always required? Our best understanding never comes from snapshots, but from time exposures. Consider the growth of a child. One of the marks which distinguish men from all the rest of creation is the long period of our immaturity when we have to learn. Almost one-third of our lives goes into slowly growing to adulthood, the years when character is formed. It takes time to become a person.

Are we then surprised that it takes time for God to make us fruitful in our suffering? If only we could learn to trust the patient processes of God! Somehow in our day we have come to believe, as our common speech has it, that we are "working against time." Yet Christians of other generations have believed they were working *with* time. They trusted it. It was on their side. They knew that "in the fulness of time," as the King James Version of the Bible called it, God would make clear what he was about. Faith is so deeply needed by some who have come up against suffering today and do not see any sense in it.

Sometimes you may waken in the middle of the night and if it is a time of distress you will long for the morning to come. By every outward evidence the darkness is there to stay. You do not see anything breaking the shadow. But the permanence of the darkness is an illusion; it is not true that it will remain. As a matter of fact, at the very moment when you lie awake after midnight, the earth is already rushing toward the morning at a speed so incredible it's imperceptible. The very hour of darkness when nothing seems to be happening is precisely the time when the whole earth is in motion, having passed the meridian and moved toward morning. You may not sense the movement, but nothing can stop that morning from coming.

So, when suffering comes and the way is dark, a similar faith can be ours. He still will make you fruitful in the land of your affliction.

3. HIGH FAILURE AND LOW SUCCESS

SOMEONE HAS SAID THAT ONE OF THE SIMPLEST WAYS TO UNDERSTAND another person is to see what he underlines when he reads a book. It seems that we read with our need. So by a kind of natural selection there are some words we reserve for ourselves. What a revelation it would be if we were to share with one another those words we choose to underline! It might be a fragment of a hymn, a portion of Scripture, or possibly something which came in a personal letter when we needed it most.

Mr. Alec Waugh, the distinguished English author, tells of such a phrase which he has remembered over the years. It was taken from a poem written at Oxford by his father. The poem itself has been lost, but a few words of it remain. Alec Waugh says they always gave him help in a time of testing. The words are these: "High failure towering o'er low success." Quite an insight! And it points to a deeper understanding of some aspects of our Christian faith.

Consider the story of the walk to Emmaus as told in the New Testament. From our perspective we look upon it as one of the days of great victory. But don't forget that it didn't seem so at the time. The men walking the road to Emmaus were under the shadow of the crucifixion. They were burdened with failure. The highest hopes they ever had known had been shattered that day by the sight of a cross on a hill. What a revealing response they gave to the unknown stranger who fell into step with them! Speaking of Christ, they said, "We had hoped that he would be the one to redeem Israel." We *had* hoped, you see. It was in the past tense. Here were men trying to get their souls around the awful fact of failure. And we've all had such times. And it takes a great faith

14

to believe that it might be high failure towering o'er low success. This is true, for example, of the *life of devotion*. Almost certainly we've known our times of failure in prayer. Like the disciples we have to ask, "Teach us to pray." And the very asking reflects, it seems to me, that we feel we've failed on our own. It was the fact that Jesus found such reality in prayer that led all those around him to see how far they had missed it.

But isn't that a high failure which towers over little success? What if the life of devotion gives us only a passing moment of the reality of God? What if we see God, as it were, but fleetingly while we see other things steadily? Isn't it better to have known him at least that much, than to have known other realities with less effort? Surely the Psalmist was right: "For a day in thy courts is better than a thousand elsewhere."

Or again I think this is a word about the church and what it must do. Let it be clear that we believe the Christian mission is supposed to succeed wherever it can. But neither can the church be judged by its low successes. Sometimes it will bear finer tribute to its Lord by its higher failures. You see, the first business of the church is reconciliation. It's overcoming the alienations of men from God and from themselves. It's mending the severed ties with one another. Reconciliation! How lightly we speak the word, yet a moment's sober thought will remind us that it's one of life's most demanding tasks, requiring all the gifts of grace we have. If we fail, as often we must, it is in part because of the sheer magnitude of the task. Our only shame is in a disobedience which does not try. For God can use even our failures as well as our achievements to the ends of the kingdom.

4. LET'S LEAP OVER A WALL

As THE EVENING CAME ON, THE TRAIN SPED ACROSS THE PLAIN OF Poland. For most of the day a group of passengers had sat in the same compartment, each contained in his own thoughts, each an island not touching the other. There was a Polish woman, two women from the Ukraine, a Czechoslovakian woman, and a French pastor. When the darkness came, the French pastor opened his New Testament and began to read his evening devotions. But as it happens for all of us, lulled by the motion of the train, he dozed for a moment in his reading, and his New Testament fell to the floor of the compartment. One of the peasant women from the Ukraine picked it up, fingered it for a moment, studied it curiously before she handed it back to the pastor. Then with a smile she reached into her own bundle and pulled out a red-bound, well worn Bible printed in Russian. She held it out so that he might see that she too had a Bible of her own. The French pastor saw his opportunity. He opened his New Testament and pointed to Ephesians 2:14, and by gesture asked her to find the same passage in her own Bible. When she found it and read the words, a smile came across her face. For the words are these: "He is our peace who has made us both one." She read the words to the others in the compartment and soon those who had sat through the day without really touching each other were nodding and smiling. After some conversation the pastor pointed to another verse. She found it in her Bible and read the words: "Grace to you and peace from God our father, and the Lord Jesus Christ."

Now that's a true story. More than that, it is a story which reminds us of an abiding truth. It is graphically expressed in the eighteenth Psalm. It is in a passage in which the Psalmist describes the power which God can bring into the life of a man. He tells how

16

Gene E. Bartlett

God can humble the haughty and support the humble; how God is a shield for those who take refuge in him; and how he sets a man in a large place and makes his feet safe and secure on the way. But right in the midst of it is an intriguing description. The psalmist says, "By my God I can leap over a wall." Well, that's the kind of verse which, once read, leaves a lasting picture in your mind. All our lives we find ourselves up against walls of one kind or another.

Prejudice, for example, is a wall in human life. The word means, of course, "prejudging," making up your mind about people by the name they bear or by their race or by the section of the country from which they came or by some rumor which has been carried to you. Whatever the form of prejudice, it builds walls. It causes Shylock to say to Bassanio, "I will buy with you, sell with you, talk with you, walk with you . . . but I will not eat with you, drink with you, nor pray with you." And there's a wall!

Equally real is the barrier in the spiritual life which men have called sin. It comes close to all of us. It causes a man like Paul to say, "For I do not do the things I want, but the evil I do not want is what I do." That's the experience of sin in human life. You haven't gone very deep in your Christian experience if you've not had to face this reality.

But, whatever the wall, there's an exhilarating sense of victory in leaping over and running free. If it is to happen it means we must take the confidence and the assurance that God does empower us to make the leap. And it means we shall never be content in heart and mind until at last we take the Psalmist's word as our own. It's time to move into the large place which God has prepared. By our God let us leap over the wall!

17

5. LED EVERY STEP OF THE WAY

IF THIS WERE THE TIME AND THE PLACE, AND THE INVITATION WERE given to share your favorite verse of Scripture, we can be sure that almost immediately someone would quote the sixth verse of the third chapter of Proverbs: "In all your ways acknowledge him, and he will make straight your paths." It's a favorite, not only because many of us learned it early in our lives, but also because it gives expression to a hope and a hunger. We find so much strength and comfort in the faith that God does direct our paths.

In these words, it seems to me, are brought together two essentials which cannot be separated. They make clear first that there is something for us to do and then that there is something God has promised to do. We may call one the *condition* of guidance and the other the *assurance* of guidance. An immature faith tries to separate these two, but let's combine them, because together they comprise the two sides of this tremendous faith in God's guidance.

First there is the *condition of guidance*. "In all your ways acknowledge him. . . ." Obviously this must be the condition of God's guidance. We cannot be led until we are ready to be!

Perhaps we can put it into a modern picture. After all, our day has its own parables as the biblical days had theirs. This came to me recently on a plane trip. We were putting into the airport in Chicago when I realized that in our landing there was a parable of guidance. Almost literally the words we are considering in this moment were being carried out in the process of bringing that plane safely in. You see, one of the requirements of safe flight is that the pilot of the plane as he approaches an airport must report to the tower and acknowledge authority to direct traffic in a given area. As the plane approaches, the pilot must report and place

18

himself under the direction of that tower. He must put his plane into the pattern as it is assigned to him. And, only as each pilot acknowledges the authority of the tower and places himself in obedience, can all the planes in the area land safely. Every hour of every day, this drama is being carried out. Two things you see — a pilot acknowledging an authority higher than himself, and in turn having his paths directed for him.

Here in a modern parable, it seems to me, is a partial picture of God's guidance of our lives. The point is that just as the pilot must acknowledge the authority of the tower before his paths can be directed for him, so any life must come to the place where it first gives obedience to God's direction. That is the condition: "In all your ways acknowledge him. . . ."

Then there is the assurance: "He shall direct thy paths." But, you say, how does God do that? It may be through a gift which he has imparted to you, or it may be in the exercise of a sound judgment which he has given you. Sometimes it is through circumstances as one door closes and another opens. Or often it is in that peace which comes in the midst of our pain.

What hope these words hold out in a day in which so many of us are drifting! They can mean joy for those who have discovered this already. They can be a special support to some who are passing through a time of testing in their lives. Can you think of anything which could mean more to young people than taking this truth at the beginning of life and living it through all their years?

It begins with simple counsel: Acknowledge him. If you really want the guidance of God, you first have to ask, "Is your back or your face toward him?"

6. PROBLEMS TRANSFORMED INTO POWER

As the years go by, we find that among our most trying hours are those times when we have to take No for an answer. In childhood it may have been something we wanted very much but could not have. In our youth it may have been the eagerness for an opportunity which never opened. In our mature years it well may be our prayer for the sparing of a loved one or the lifting of a personal burden. Whenever No is the answer to our most earnest plea, our faith is severely tried.

I do not profess to have an easy answer to such a time. The problem is too deep and the mystery lies at last in the mind and heart of God alone. But there are some times of insight which suggest a working faith for the hours when life says No. Stated most simply, it is the belief that problems which remain in your life actually may be transformed into a source of new power. Is that why God allows them to remain? I don't know. But the fact that these often become the points of victory seems very clear.

There is an interesting insight in the well-known story of Jesus' healing of the man who came to him carried on a pallet by his friends. When at last the paralyzed man, lowered through the roof of the house, was confronted by Jesus, the first act was to set him free by forgiveness. But when the people murmured because Christ claimed to forgive sin, there was a subsequent and a very human scene. Which is easier, asked Jesus, to say that a man's sin is forgiven or to tell him to take up his bed and walk? And to show the people his power he told this man to take up his bed and walk.

Sometimes I wonder if we would have argued with the Master at this point. Can't you imagine some of us saying, "But Master, why do I have to take up that bed? Why can't I just walk? I've been on that thing long enough! I don't want to have anything more to do with it. Can't I just leave that behind?" But here's the strange fact. The record goes on to say that the man rose immediately and took up the bed and walked. So, you see, the very symbol of his weakness had become the sign of his power. That upon which he had lain imprisoned had become the mark of his victory.

Now what is deepest here is the confidence that in all these things God is working his own purpose. Essentially that is the hope Jesus held out to us again and again. It's the confidence which led Paul, having prayed three times for release from his problem, at last to accept No for an answer and to know that God, while not removing the problem, would give him grace to carry it. "My grace is sufficient for you." That's what Paul learned.

Can we really believe this in the times when God says No and we see a difficult way ahead? Is God's purpose still there? Samuel Taylor Coleridge, who has given us some of the hymns we cherish, wrote a letter in the last months of his life to a young friend. At that time he had been confined to his room for three or four years, but this is what he wrote: "For the last four years I have been, with brief intervals, confined to a sick room, hopeless of recovery. Thus on the very brink of death I solemnly bear witness to you that the Almighty Redeemer is faithful to perform what He has promised and has preserved under all my pains and infirmities the inward peace that passes understanding."

What an assurance to carry through all the changes of our lives! Our problems can be made powers when faith opens the way.

21

7. THE MOST STUBBORN QUESTION IN ANY LIFE

WE MAY BE SURE THAT THERE WOULD BE MANY OPINIONS AS TO THE most stubborn question in any life. Some of practical turn of mind would insist that it's finding the money for this month's bills! And certainly that's always with us. Others, drawing upon daily experience, might insist that the most stubborn question is how to get along with people who rub you the wrong way. Any answer, you see, will reflect the experience from which it comes.

Now, the apostle Paul had his own answer to that question. His problem was that in spite of every effort he didn't do what he ought to do. He had a conscience as big as the world itself. But he found himself repeatedly unable to live up to it. So in one of the most impassioned passages in all his letters he cried of himself: "I do not understand my own actions. For I do not do what I want, but I do the very thing I hate." Does that sound familiar? If that were a mirror, would you see any well-known reflections in it?

Now, to face that stubborn question in any life, the Christian faith offers us two great insights.

First is the fact that we all need help in handling these destructive forces in life. That's not something of which we are ashamed or something to be denied. It may not come to all of us in the same way, yet each of us feels the need for help outside himself. That's just part of being human.

Where that point of stubborn resistance — where you do the things you had willed *not* to do — may be in your life, I really can't say. But somewhere it is there. We all are up against those powerful forces. Some may feel it at the point of anger. In spite of your best resolutions, you find your wrath taking over and disrupting your inner life and your personal relationships. Or it may be in what the Bible calls lust. Your mind says one thing but the body insists on something else. So a person finds himself driven by a sensuality which he does not understand but which seems to threaten his well-being.

Far more subtle than these are those special stresses of the spirit. Consider jealousy, for example. A story comes out of the Middle

Ages relating that the tempter wanted to bring the downfall of a famous saint. So one by one he confronted him with all the things which were supposed to be tempting — sensual and material. He offered him great possessions, but that didn't bother the saint. He promised him sensual pleasures, but they could not prevail. At last the tempter tried one more thing. He whispered in the ear of the saint, "By the way, have you heard that your brother has been made Bishop of Alexandria?" What other things could not do, jealousy accomplished, and the tempter won the day.

Perhaps it is the discovery of the realities of these things which we cannot handle without help which prompted one of our poets to pen some lines one day as he was seated in a restaurant and saw the sadness of the people at the bar. He said:

> Faces along the bar
> Cling to their average day:
> The lights must never go out,
> The music must always play . . .
>
> Lest we should see where we are,
> Lost in a haunted wood,
> Children afraid of the night
> Who have never been happy or good.[1]

But the second insight is the belief that God has promised and provided the help which gives us victory. Paul starts out by saying, "I do not understand my own action." But he ends by saying, "Thanks be to God!" It was that faith which gave him the answer. What do those words mean? We believe that it is in Christ that God has given us the means of answering that most stubborn question in any life, the struggle between things as they are and as they ought to be. By God's help even that question can find its answer.

[1] W. H. Auden, "September 1, 1939," *The Collected Poetry of W. H. Auden* (New York: Random House © 1940 by W. H. Auden) p. 58. Used by permission.

8. TIMES WHEN WE NEED INNER QUIET

MOST OF US WOULD FEEL A KINSHIP WITH THE MAN WHO CAME home one evening weary after a hectic day and dropped himself into the nearest chair. "Now," he said to his wife, "I know why they call it the human *race*. Believe me that's what it is from morning till night — a race." But he added, "On second thought I'm not sure it's always human."

In such a time the sixty-second Psalm speaks to one of the deepest needs of men. Every Psalm, like a hymn, was meant for a particular occasion or conditon. The sixty-second Psalm is an affirmation of confidence for those who are being tested. It's an honest writing, for it reflects the battle in every life. There is a recurring theme containing the central word the Psalmist wants to give us. It is a word calling a man to confidence in God. Dr. Moffatt has translated the verse thus: "Leave it all quietly to God, my soul . . . rock, rescue, refuge, he is all to me." In the hurry of modern times and the stress under which most of us live, these words arouse both a hunger and a hope.

First, God is our rock. I know that's poetry! That's the only way we can speak of the deepest things. We have to look around us and find some picture to express the real experience. And men often have spoken of God as rock. So we lay hold upon this everyday experience and its picture to catch the stability, the permanence, the strength which men find in him.

In a time of great change the knowledge that God is enduring is a source of strength to all of us. Sometimes that discovery is in our personal lives. Henry Lyte gave us one of our most cherished hymns from that kind of situation. He had left his home, England,

24

and had gone to Italy seeking the recovery of his health, for he was suffering from tuberculosis. But when it became clear what the end was to be, Lyte wrote the hymn we sing so often to strengthen our faith. And it includes these words, "Change and decay in all around I see; O Thou, who changest not, abide with me!" You can't miss the witness of those words. When all else was passing, there was the certain knowledge that God was like a rock, a place to stand which was certain and sure and unchanging.

Again the Psalmist says God is our rescue. It shows how utterly realistic is the Christian view about the nature of life. It doesn't close our eyes to the fact that men come to conditions where they need to be rescued. None of us evades those points.

Thomas à Kempis, who gave us the classic devotional writing, *The Imitation of Christ*, lived for seventy years in a monastery. That's about as serene and secure a setting as any man could want. But Thomas à Kempis had to add, "Not to feel any disturbance belongs not to this life." Well, I should say it doesn't! We all have to handle the things that disturb us. There is no real inner peace this side of those human struggles.

Rock, rescue — and finally, says the Psalmist, refuge. We can give up once and for all any false idea that seeking refuge is somehow a sign of weakness. There is an honesty about this Psalm in confessing that everyone needs a place of refuge where he may be renewed for the struggle of life.

This indeed is a word of assurance, and it can be ours in this hour. It means that the times when we deeply need inner quiet are precisely the hours when God invites us back to him.

25

9. MAKING THE MOST OF THINGS

FOR SOME OF US TIME HAS NOT DIMMED THE STORY OF CAPTAIN KURT Carlsen. He was that sea captain, you remember, who stayed so valiantly by his ship off the coast of England some years ago when the ship broke in the middle. He ordered all passengers and crew into lifeboats. But according to the tradition of the sea he, as captain, stayed with the ship. Moreover he almost brought it into shore by himself. For a week he fought the seas and the sinking ship while the world stood by and watched a man put up a tremendous battle. He was trying to make the most of a very bad situation. Though we must record unfortunately that he did not at last succeed in bringing in his ship, he still left a record of courage which we'll long remember.

Perhaps one reason we remember him is that there are times in every life which seem caught up in that picture. How often we have to make the most of a bad situation! The question is whether we have the courage to do it. We set out in life, for example, having one idea what our journey is to be. Then come the unexpected circumstances or the troubles which change the whole direction. There are few spiritual crises quite as intense as these. It takes spiritual resources to make the most of things.

Yet this was part of God's word to the early church. It was no respectable thing to be a Christian in the days of the Roman Empire. The book of Revelation, for example, was written to people who really were up against it. They faced persecution and often death. The words were written to strengthen men and women trying to make the most of those circumstances. So in the seven letters to the seven churches there is included in the third chapter of Revelation this counsel: "Be watchful, and strengthen the things which remain." That's the way the King James Version has it.

26

Dr. Goodspeed has brought out the vividness of the original language in his translation: "Wake up, and strengthen what is left." Though that counsel was born centuries ago in circumstances foreign to our experience, it has something to say to our generation and to our personal needs.

We surely will be coming close to some intimate needs in the remembering of those words. There are circumstances of life which make us ready for that counsel. For example, there is illness which means that you find your physical resources cut down and you have to make the most of it. Or there are times of failure, some of them personal and moral, when a man looks out on the wreckage of his life and wonders what on earth he can make of it.

Equally true is the experience of bereavement, when the summons no man can deny comes into the family circle, and we literally have to strengthen what is left. These are hours of great spiritual testing, and the outcome is determined by whether we concentrate on what's lost or what's left. Words like these may be God's own counsel in many a personal situation today. "Wake up, and strengthen what is left."

Now this kind of approach doesn't stand by itself. If this seems to you a kind of platitude calling upon you to buck up under difficult circumstances or to keep your chin up, I shall have failed to make clear what I want to say. For you see these words do not stand by themselves. If they are only a kind of proverb, they are like a violinist practicing a solo by himself with no orchestra. But to hear these words as they ought to be heard is to hear the violinist with the whole orchestra behind him, because behind these words is the whole Christian faith. "Wake up, and strengthen what is left." That's the God-centered view of times of testing.

10. EXCEPT YOUR BROTHER BE WITH YOU

MANY A SUNDAY IN MY BOYHOOD I WENT HOME CLUTCHING ONE OF the colorful Sunday School pictures given me as a reminder of the morning's lesson. And many of you must have similar memories. For some reason one picture which I have remembered over the years was a highly idealized and colorful version of Joseph receiving his brothers in Egypt. There he stood with all the evidence of power around him while his brothers, hungry and needy and searching for food, bowed before him. That picture has stayed over these years as a reminder that of all the stories of the Old Testament none has had more continual fascination for Bible readers than that of Joseph.

It wasn't, however, until later years, that one sentence in that story began to stand out with special significance. It's the word which Joseph's brothers carried back to their father when they returned home. Joseph had sent them back because one of the brothers, Benjamin, was not with them. So they returned to their father and said, "The man said to us, 'You shall not see my face unless your brother is with you.'"

Now I suppose to lift those words out of their original setting and let them stand by themselves is an audacious thing to do, but I am going to do it. For it seems to me they are a remarkable expression of an essential Christian truth. It is as though God himself addressed those words to us. "You shall not see my face, unless your brother is with you." That's a summary of one of the most constant teachings of Jesus, namely that one does not love God who cannot love his brother. To say it another way, the most tangible evidence of our love of God is the way we treat our brother.

Brotherhood itself is not necessarily a distinction. It is enjoying a great popularity. Everyone's for it in some form or other, by their own definition. It is even possible to have brotherhood of a certain kind that has no relation at all to our search for God. Thomas Hardy was a skeptic and a man of poignant searching, but he had a great compassion. Those who knew him best remember how he took care of the prisoners of war who were stationed near his home in Britain. Yet Thomas Hardy had brotherhood without any sense of relationship to God, a fact he confessed with sadness.

But the Christian faith, on the other hand, ties those two things together. It makes it clear that our brotherhood is a special kind. It comes because we are under the good news that God has first loved us, and therefore we must love our brother. The very heart of the Christian faith is that we must do unto others as God in Christ already has done unto us. Moreover, we know where to begin in our search for God. A man has to look no farther than his brother who stands beside him.

If the Christian faith affirmed that God is available only to those who have some special esthetic sensitivity or some great intellectual capacity, it would close the door to many of us. But, *everyone* has to stand with his brother, and the Christian faith says *that's* the point at which you begin in your search for God. Begin doing what love requires toward your brother, and the day will come when you will feel that God has opened his way to you and you've come to know him. That's the word which comes with special meaning: God says, "You shall not see my face, unless your brother is with you."

11. WHEN LIFE CRUMBLES AT THE CORE

In November of 1936 one of the most amazing women of our time, Helen Keller, passed through an hour of great personal sadness. Her cherished friend and teacher, Anne Sullivan, had died. This was more than the loss of a friend. For, you see, it was Anne Sullivan who had rescued Helen as a child from the darkness and imprisonment of a life without the ability to see and hear. With great patience she had reached the imprisoned child and set her free through the power to communicate with others by the sense of touch.

Then in 1936, Anne Sullivan died. Helen Keller has described her feeling of utter desolation. She said that the days after that were "like a glacier over a field once joyously green." But today Helen Keller continues her work, a radiant, living witness to the triumph of faith over darkness. Shortly after her beloved teacher's death she set out for Scotland with a new companion. Of Helen Keller in that hour the biographer says, "Feeling that life is a wonderful game she was bent on playing it out to the very end convinced that courage is the cure for every sorrow." When life was threatened at the core, Helen Keller won her personal victory.

So real are those hours which come to us all in some way or other that the ancient Psalmist framed a question. He asked, "If the foundations are destroyed, what can the righteous do?" Well, to some that question seems a long way from today's need, but for others of us that may be exactly the question we are facing. Our lives are described by the poet Yeats: "Things fall apart, the center cannot hold." What answer do we have to the Psalmist's question?

The Christian faith has profound insight. First, it says, open your life to God from now on. If the door has been closed, then keep it closed on the past, but open it for the future. Do it as deliberately and consciously as you would open the door to a friend whom you want to know and to whom you would say, "Come live here. Let me live my life with you." Now, the Christian life is just like that, opening your own mind and life to Jesus Christ. Know everything about him that you can. And one of the most amazing truths is that you will never come to a place where there isn't more to know. That's a fact! At first you may think we know so little about him. Then you begin to enter into his faith, his thoughts, the meaning of his life, his temptations, his victory, his triumph over death. You'll want to know more as long as you live, and there's always more to know. Make your decision, then, to open your life to every knowledge of him you can gain. Let him throw light on every experience. Cultivate his presence in the hours of your devotion, and you will find that he becomes a *new* center at the point where the old has crumbled. That's the first thing.

The second thing is to find fellowship with others in the Christian faith. There's nothing splendid about being solitary. The fact that life requires the help of others is not a sign of weakness, but of strength.

As I say this, I recall a time when certain words of another person took on great meaning in my own life. They were written by G. A. Studdert-Kennedy. Once in a dark place of his life he put his feelings into these lines:

> These clouds are lies.
> They cannot last. The blue sky is the Truth.
> For God is Love. Such is my Faith, and such
> My reasons for it, and I find them strong
> Enough. And you? You want to argue? Well,
> I can't. It's a choice. I choose the Christ.[1]

May you choose him, too, and find new foundation at the very point where life has crumbled at the core.

[1] "Faith," *The Sorrows of God* (New York: Harper & Row © 1924).

31

12. SECOND THOUGHTS
ARE BETTER THAN THE FIRST

OUT OF THE TRAGEDY OF WAR A PHRASE WAS BORN. IT WAS FIRST heard in those opening unbelievable months of the Pacific conflict when defeat followed defeat. To summarize the cause of these setbacks someone framed the phrase, "Too little and too late."

Well, even after these years those words have endured. Possibly it is because they seem to express a discouragement with which we are tempted at crucial points in our lives. Most of us, for example, contrast the actual achievements of our lives with our original intentions and we have to confess "too little." Others of us remember the intellectual discipline we once set for ourselves in our search for knowledge, and, noting how often it has been interrupted and distracted, we conclude "too little." Or there is the life of prayer. Most of us know promptings and stirrings which lead us to hope that we too may center down in God, but we discover as the years go by that it's "too little." Somewhere then, you see, it touches us all in our capacity to love, our usefulness in our vocation, or our hunger for personal fulfillment. Too little! Then is it really too late?

The question hardly has been formed before the Bible goes to work to offer its answer. It calls up witnesses, retells events, puts its faith into poetry, and, at last, rests its case on the belief that God has made himself known in Christ so that we may see the word in the flesh.

One of the most vivid affirmations is in a story which we often counted of minor importance, the narrative of Jonah. Unfortunately we have not done justice to Jonah — we've been so fascinated by his means of transportation that we haven't looked at his means of grace!

Well, let's look at it for a moment. The story is told with a superb economy of language. The word of God comes to Jonah commanding him to go to the city of Nineveh to proclaim judgment. But who wants to carry a word of judgment? Not Jonah! He heads in the opposite direction, "fleeing from the presence of the Lord," as the narrator says. Then things happen quickly. In the swiftly moving story Jonah goes off to Joppa, steps on board ship — and straight into a storm. In the superstition of those times men caught in a storm supposed that someone had offended God. Discovering that Jonah was in flight from God, they see no other course but to toss the poor man overboard in order that others might be saved. Then it is that the renowned great fish keeps its appointment with Jonah, swallows him up, and delivers him after three days to, of all places, the shores of Nineveh.

And here the word comes with a blend of insight and humor. It says, "The word of the Lord came to Jonah the second time, saying, 'Arise, go to Nineveh.'"

So some of our greatest experiences and our most far-reaching decisions are made when the word of God does come a second time. T. R. Glover has even marked this as one of the chief encounters of a man with God. Said Glover, "The Son of Man comes to us in queer shapes and forms, in new duties and I think particularly in the distasteful duty of thinking things through again." Sometimes God's second word is a command calling us to a neglected duty. Sometimes it's a word of comfort calling us out of our sorrow. And almost always it's an invitation to a fuller life than we yet have found.

This matter is so intimate and so profound that no hope like this should be held out if the ground of our faith doesn't support it. But the good news is *addressed* to life and *attested* by life and it tells us that the word *does* come a second time. It may be too little, but it is not too late.

Roger Fredrikson . . . is pastor of the First Baptist Church of Sioux Falls, South Dakota, and chairman of the Board of Managers of the American Baptist Board of Education and Publication. At one time, he headed the Department of Religion and Philosophy at Ottawa University in Kansas. Other posts of service have included First Vice President of the American Baptist Convention, National President of the Baptist Youth Fellowship, delegate and speaker to various world-wide youth conferences, and pastor of the First Baptist Church of Ottawa.

13. ON BEING SALT

It stood there on the table, small and insignificant — just a salt shaker. A moment before, I had used it to sprinkle a bit of salt on my eggs for breakfast. Interesting. What good could small, white crystals be to eggs? Yet I wouldn't care to eat much of anything without some salt on it. Would you? It's amazing how such insignificant looking stuff as salt could be so important.

Did you know that once upon a time salt was one of the most costly commodities to men? It still is. Now, why is that? Well, offhand, there are at least two reasons. First, salt brings flavor and seasoning to food. Otherwise the food is flat and tasteless. Second, salt preserves much that is perishable. To put it bluntly, salt keeps food from rotting. So salt has a crucial work to do. Now, of course salt can't do its work at all if it is kept in the shaker. After a while the taste and power of the salt would be gone. This is why salt is good only when it is scattered. It must come into contact with the meat or bread if it is to bring taste or do its preserving. So we cast this insignificant-looking stuff on the food, and it disappears as far as the eye can tell. Then it quietly does its effective work. It literally dies so the food can live.

What a marvelous analogy that Jesus should say to his disciples that they were the salt of the earth! How do we become salt?

36

Roger Fredrikson

Well a disciple is someone who has come to sit at the feet of Jesus. He is there to learn, to become Christlike. The disciple is the kind of person who is poor in spirit, who is meek, who is merciful and pure in heart. He may even be persecuted for doing the right thing. Anyone of us who is serious at all about being a Christian will stay close enough to Christ to grow in these great qualities.

It is peculiar and tragic how we want to keep the salt in shakers. We keep gathering Sunday after Sunday in church buildings and do our worshiping and teaching and getting inspired. Then when the meeting is over we somehow imagine that the job is done. This is why we lose our taste, and even end up becoming completely ineffective. We will never be true to our calling by staying in the shaker. The power of the Christian community, when it is true to itself, is that it dares to be scattered for the sake of Christ and his world.

In the mystery of the spirit the life of Christ can be brought into all areas of life — the school, the home, our work, and a thousand other places — if we are truly disciples. There are homes and places of work that have been changed radically by an obedience to Christ. My friend, you can be salt bringing flavor and change and salvation into life wherever you are. You are called to be salt.

14. FISHING ON THE OTHER SIDE

FISHING IS A GLORIOUS AND FRUSTRATING CHALLENGE. HAVE YOU EVER had the experience of spending half a day or so fishing in one place and not catching a thing, then moving just a few feet, throwing in the line, and all of a sudden having the fish start to bite? I will have to confess to that humiliating experience of catching nothing on the right side of the boat, using what I thought was top grade tackle and highly advertised bait, while our eleven-year-old son was catching bluegills or crappies one after another from the other side using makeshift equipment. That can be pretty frustrating.

There is a story in the Gospel of John that deals with this kind of strange business in fishing. It tells how a band of discouraged disciples decided to go back to their fishing. These disciples had given themselves, as best they knew how, to following Jesus. His teachings and way of life had made a deep claim on their lives. They had come to believe in his kingdom. Now, it was all over. He had been crucified. Their whole world had come crashing in around their heads, and in the midst of the broken hopes they turned back toward Galilee. Here were the familiar haunts, their old weather-beaten boats, and their worn nets. Here was a life they knew and understood. Why listen to the strange music of a kingdom that now seemed completely unreal when you could go back to the practical, real work of fishing? So all through the night they fished, but they caught nothing. Even in this old life of fishing, there was frustration and disappointment.

Then in the morning, just as day was breaking, a voice came through the mist: "Children have you any fish?" Imagine their almost hostile answer, "Of course not." Then the voice told them to cast the net on the other side and they would get a catch. What a ridiculous idea! What right did a stranger have to come along and ask experienced fishermen to cast their nets in a different place? But in their weary frustration they obeyed. And, now, an amazing thing took place. There were fish on that side of the boat—such a catch that they could not haul in the net. It was Peter, the big fisherman, who then cried out with amazed joy, "It is the Lord!" Indeed it was. This was the resurrected Christ coming back to be with his disciples.

Friends, you and I have fished too long on the wrong side of the boat. We have lived by doubt when we should have lived in faith. We have been steeped with cynicism when we should have launched out in love. We have been tremendously aware of the problems and not at all certain of any answers. And, in our imagined self-sufficiency, we have fooled ourselves into believing that we knew where to fish. When someone has tried to suggest another place, we become stubborn. "After all," our argument has run, "we are realists," and so we continue in our night of fear.

Ah, but there is a voice, there is a word that comes from one who has been through death and now invites us to dare believe in a new way. Some men say this talk of Christ and resurrection is an illusion. But it is the testimony of a living church that Christ is alive and that he offers men victory over darkness and frustration. Do we dare try the other side of the boat? This is a way of faith and a new beginning. It is the way of trust and becoming as a child. It is the way of love and open doors. This is the side of the boat where Christ's answer waits for us.

15. BECOMING FISHERS OF MEN

HAVE YOU EVER TRIED FISHING FOR BASS? AFTER BEING A KIND OF amateur fisherman for some years, I learned last summer something of the technique to be used if bass are going to be caught. It was one of those lovely Minnesota evenings when the lake was smooth as glass. I happened to come upon a fisherman who obviously knew what he was doing. He kept casting his frog into the rushes right up near the shore, in a casual sort of way. While he did this with one hand, he kept working the oar with the other — and all the time he was keeping the boat at an easy distance from the shore.

Since this fisherman didn't seem to resent my impolite intrusion, we chatted about bass fishing. I plied him with questions: When is the best time to go after these fish? Where do you find them? What are their feeding habits? He was very generous in sharing his best knowledge. All of this opened a full new experience in fishing for me, trying to catch the wily bass.

It has always been interesting that the main core of Jesus' disciples were men who fished for a living. One can see the wisdom of Jesus in choosing these men. Think of what their trade had taught them! These were men who understood the ways of nature and the mystery of the sea. They were at home in God's world.

Roger Fredrikson

Their livelihood depended on knowing the habits of the fish and the seasons for catching them. These were men who were not afraid of loneliness and who knew the patience of long waiting.

It was to men like these that Jesus laid down his challenge: "Follow me, and I will make you fishers of men." Jesus asked for the fishing wisdom and patience of these men that it might be used to bring other men into his great kingdom.

What we need today is a new generation of fishermen — not those who will go after fish, but those who will go after men in the name of Christ. We need men who will let Christ teach them how to fish. He will share with us the passion of his great heart of love, and then this love can touch other men. Can we find men who will see with Christ's eyes the possibilities of every person becoming a child of God? Will there be those who will have the patience to love, hope, and wait when there seems to be no return on the investment?

There are many of us who are busy with our own fishing tackle. We are doing a hundred important, worthwhile things, but we are not doing the *one great thing* — following Christ that we may become "fishers of men."

We invite you to that kind of fishing.

16. COMING IN ON THE BEAM

SOME TIME AGO I HAD OCCASION TO SPEND SEVERAL HOURS IN THE Philadelphia International Airport waiting to catch a late plane. During that time I met a naval officer who knew a great deal about the Philadelphia Airport. So we had the opportunity of visiting what is really the nerve center of a modern, well-equipped airport — its control tower. Here are the men and women who, with the use of radar and radio, guide the gleaming monsters that we call airliners onto the right runways. What a crucial business these people are engaged in! I stood amazed, listening to the babble of talk involving many planes and many operators in that control tower. Each operator was a study in concentration as he watched his planes on the radar screens and gave the instructions to the different pilots. These were highly skilled, sensitive people who are really the heroes of modern aviation. Somehow in the midst of all the activity the right planes managed to get onto the right runways at the right time.

Early the next morning our plane was finally landing at the airport in Chicago. It had been a long, foggy night, and now our pilots circled the field time after time before finally bringing us onto the runway. All during those minutes there was a picture of that control tower in my mind. I wondered who was keeping lonely vigil in the control tower at that hour of the morning. How amazing that the skills and dedication of many people were focused on a single plane that it might come in safely through the darkness of the night!

Roger Fredrikson

Now, if this is possible with man, how much more with God! There are some of us who take a dim view of the possibility of God's providential care. Yet we accept without question the accomplishments of men in electronics and radio. One of the great convictions of our faith is that there is a personal God who is concerned with the personal affairs of each man. It is this God who is aware when a sparrow falls to the ground and who cares for a single, lovely lily. The whole of Jesus' life and ministry was a witness to that wondrous care of his Father. Even in the hour of cruel death Jesus could say: "Father, into thy hands I commit my spirit."

Often when I go to prayer, I remember the picture of the control tower which is like a parable of prayer to me. There is a vast, infinite, personal God in whom I rest myself. He loves us and cares for us at all times. He knows us by name and understands all our needs. If earthly parents, who are not perfect, know how to care for their children's needs, how much more does our Heavenly Father, who is perfect, know how to give us all that we need. To use the language of the airport, he knows which runway we should come in on, and he will bring us in if we let him.

When we kneel in prayer we are asking for guidance and help to come in on the right beam. The final petition of all prayer is "Thy kingdom come, thy will be done." To open one's inmost self to the impulses and love of the Heavenly Father is to enter into one of life's greatest adventures. In the midst of the fog and the darkness he can bring us in on the right beam.

17. GRAVEL IN HIS CHARACTER

THERE IS A POWERFUL PICTURE IN THE OLD TESTAMENT OF A CHARacter named Samson. In many ways he was a fierce, awesome, courageous man, but in other ways he was like a little child. This man was given a great task by God. He was to be one of the judges of Israel and would use his mighty strength and cunning to defeat the Philistines. Long before he was born, his parents made a vow dedicating this child to God. It may seem strange to us, but the symbol of that vow was that his hair would never be cut.

The early part of Samson's life was filled with great conquests. There is the account of how he picked up the gates of a city and carried them off; of how he killed hundreds of men with the jawbone of an ass; and how he spread fire through the wheat fields of the Philistines by tying fire brands to the tails of foxes. So, terror and fear spread through the camp of Israel's enemy. There was nothing the Philistines could do to stop Samson by meeting him head-on in open battle. He simply pushed on, leaving the enemy in the shambles of defeat wherever he went. He was God's giant.

However, if a man cannot be brought down by a frontal attack, perhaps he can be struck through the back door. This is what happened to Samson. The beginning of his downfall was an unholy alliance with a woman who did not belong to his own people. Delilah was a beautiful, seductive creature whose basic loyalty was not to Samson, but to the Philistines. So, using all the wiles at her command, she attempted to gain the secret of Samson's strength. Delilah went through all the moods — petulance, warmth, anger, and all the rest — to learn of the giant's massive strength, and each time Samson fooled her. Finally, she got to him, and he told her the secret of his hair. One day while he was sleeping, his head was shorn and his strength departed; Samson was just another man.

The ending of Samson's life was a sad, disgraceful picture of a great hulk of a man, now blinded by the enemy and forced to grind their mills. It is only in one last desperate surge of strength after a pitiful cry to his God that Samson pulls down the pillars of the Temple of Dagon and brings thousands of the Philistines with him to death.

One cannot read this story without a deep sense of sorrow. Here is tremendous promise and strength, but here is also fatal weakness, and the downfall comes through that weakness. There is not a one of us who does not have gravel in his character or clay in his feet. To assume that we are self-sufficient can be the beginning of our undoing. Temptations or weaknesses do not walk up to the front door and ask to come in. The enemies are in the basement waiting for the right moment. We are in the greatest danger when we assume we have the greatest strength. But when a man remembers that his strength comes from the Lord and that in dependence on him there is lasting security, then God will guard him from all evil, and the battle will be won.

The evil that finally masters us begins in carelessness. We feel that church attendance is relatively unimportant. We say we will pray when we feel like it. We evade the Christian fellowship. Finally, there comes a day when we do not care at all. We may even ridicule the sacred facts of our faith. The unholy alliance has gotten us caught like a fly on sticky paper. It is a sad but all too common story that people with great potential, who once claimed to love Christ, can end up in the temple of the false gods grinding the mills blindly in desperation. The only hope in even that hour is the providence and grace of God. May we be granted the wisdom and humility to lean on the only one who is our final strength.

45

18. FACING THE CENTER

On the back side of the great Rushmore Memorial in the
Black Hills of South Dakota is a lovely camp called Judson.
Throughout the summer months young people and families and
groups of men and women gather to share with Christ in life's
deep, yet simple, experiences in this camp. The hills ring with the
laughter of play and the thoughtful words of prayer and study. A
week of Christian camping is an unforgettable experience of growth,
love, and challenge. Anyone who has passed through this kind
of week can testify to its rich meaning.

Now at Judson, as in many other such camps, the last experience
of the day is always the circle of fellowship around a blazing camp-
fire. This is the climax of all the events of every wonderful day. It
is a great sight to see campers, some hand in hand, and their coun-
selors coming from every area of the grounds to join in the singing,
the simple sharing, and the prayer that close the day. There is a
sense of eagerness and anticipation in everyone's coming. All of
us are responding to the call of the ringing bell to come out of the
darkness and join together around the light and warmth of a fire.
This is an experience of facing the center, and the wonder is that
here we also face each other.

Roger Fredrikson

Do you know that this is a meaningful parable of the whole Christian faith? There is a Spirit that calls us out of darkness to face a light and warmth which glows at the center of life. Christ is like a great fire in the midst of the cold darkness. He is the Light, says the Apostle John, that overcomes the darkness. When we live with our backs to this center, we face only the uncertainty and loneliness of a bleak darkness. But, when we turn away from the darkness toward that center, we discover light and warmth which is the offer of hope, fellowship, and love.

More than that — in turning to face the fire we discover the *others* who have also found that center. The Christian community is a fellowship of people who face each other and who are united in love around a common center. This is stated beautifully by another writer in the New Testament: "Once you were no people but now you are God's people." So, every time I stand with the others in that circle of love around that fire at Camp Judson, I am filled with gratitude for that great light which came into the world that we might discover each other in him. The Spirit is calling us like the chimes of a bell to join God's people who have found their hope and life in Christ.

19. OUTSIDE THE CAMP

WE SOMETIMES HAVE THE MISTAKEN NOTION THAT RELIGION IS A NICE, safe affair that belongs only inside the church building. So many of us subconsciously associate talk of God and prayer with nice, pious people. This may be a form of religion, but it is not the Christian faith.

There is a magnificent, gripping statement in one of the epistles of the New Testament which says: "So Jesus also suffered outside the gate in order to sanctify the people through his own blood. Therefore, let us go forth to him outside the camp, bearing abuse for him." I can think of no statement that underlines more bluntly the fact that Christ and his people belong right in the middle of all that life is. Over and over again one is impressed that Jesus did his mightiest work right out in the hurly-burly of life. In fact, he was so much a part of people and their experiences that men called him a wine-bibber and a glutton, and when he died they hung him up at the Place of the Skull, not in a church sanctuary, and this was little more than a garbage pile. This was a place so much a part of the world that the simple statement "He was the King of the Jews" had to be written in the three great languages of the day. He died where men swore and gambled for his seamless robe. This was a place of vulgarity and it was this that Christ had come to redeem. The Epistle says it was "outside the gate."

Roger Fredrikson

Now, as Christ's people, we are called to join him there outside the camp. The witness of Christ belongs where housewives must deal with the daily frustrations and burdens of the children and home. The witness belongs where men use whiskey to move a product or where they cheat on their expense accounts. Christ asks us to join him on the assembly lines, in the halls of politics, and in the daily struggle of all men to earn their daily bread. This is where we Christians will win or lose the battle for Christ — outside the camp.

Something of the whole meaning of this was thrust upon me one night in the closing of a youth camp. Some of the young people and one of their leaders had fashioned a cross from fallen trees which they had anchored high on a craggy hill outside the camp. In the dark of the night this same group had climbed back up on this hill with lights. As the rest of us softly sang hymns of the cross back in camp, the lights went on the cross. Then in the silence the words came echoing over the valley, "He was wounded for our transgressions, he was bruised for our iniquities." It was an unforgettable moment. If the Christian church is to be worth its salt, it must join Christ in healing love at the place where the world is wounded and bruised. We are invited to join him outside the camp.

49

20. THE POWER OF A GREAT FINISH

SOME YEARS AGO A CERTAIN YOUNG MAN FAILED TO MAKE THE Olympic Team. His name was Buddy Edelen. He was a great track star at Washington High School and later at the University of Minnesota, but this wasn't enough to put him on the Olympic Team which went to Rome in 1960. Out of the ashes of that defeat came the joy of victory, for Buddy Edelen became the first American to win a birth on the next Olympic Team, which went to Tokyo in 1964. Buddy runs the Marathon, the most historic of all track events. It originated in Greece almost twenty-five hundred years ago, when a man ran 22 miles, 1,470 yards from Marathon to Athens, carrying the news of victory in battle.

After his defeat Buddy Edelen began to prepare, in the style of champions, for the Tokyo Olympics. He went to England to teach school so that he could compete in the great distance races of Europe. All of his life was gathered around a rigorous training program to prepare himself for victory. He ran an average of 130 miles a week. In a press interview he indicated that he has a heartbeat of 36 per minute — the deliberate slowdown which comes to all endurance athletes. He ran with four or five sweat shirts to prepare himself for competing in hot weather, and it was in 90° heat that Buddy ran the Marathon distance twenty minutes faster than his nearest competitor. His time that day was 2 hours, 24 minutes, 25.6 seconds. This is the power of a great finish!

Life is full of people who start well but never finish. All about

50

us there is the wreckage of people who began a race, but after the first defeat folded up and crawled home. This is true in marriage. It is true of people who go to school, and it is certainly true in the Christian life. So many of us start jobs we never finish. Most anyone can run a flashy first lap, but the question is: Who will be making the big push on the last lap?

Over and over again, Jesus spoke of people counting the cost before they set out to do something. He said, "For which of you, desiring to build a tower, does not first sit down and count the cost, whether he has enough to complete it?" When people came to him with easy excuses or fast talk, he always spoke direct truth with them. Perhaps his classic statement was: "If any man would come after me, let him deny himself and take up his cross and follow me." He was calling for the power of a great finish. So we need people who will not only begin to pray but who will end their lives with prayer. We need strong men and women who will not only start with a Sunday School class or some church job, because of a flashy inspiration, but who will stay with the class or the job when the going is rough, because Christ bids them go all the way.

When the apostle Paul had to stand up and make a defense for his life before a king, he was able to say, after recounting his conversion experience, "I was not disobedient to the heavenly vision." It's that kind of finish to which Christ invites us.

21. THE TRAGEDY OF THE QUITTERS

ONE OF THE TRAGEDIES OF OUR TIME IS THE HIGH SCHOOL DROPOUT. This is the young person who for any of a half dozen reasons simply falls by the wayside in his school experience. Most of the time, however, a young person quits because the school experience has no meaning for him. He has no interest in the subjects, and he has constructed the kind of world in which he believes education is not a necessity. Here is the tragedy of wasted manpower, the loss of a tremendous natural resource.

But have you ever stopped to think that the spiritual dropout is an even more frightening loss? In the New Testament there is a strange and tragic story which slips in between the lines in the experience of the apostle Paul. One of his working companions was a man named Demas. On a number of occasions Paul included this name in a greeting which usually came at the end of each of his letters. Demas was a partner in the service of Christ. Then, in what was probably his last letter, Paul said, "Demas, in love with this present world, has deserted me and gone to Thessalonica." This unhappy word of failure comes out of a Roman jail when Paul needs all the help he can muster.

At first one wonders how a man who traveled with Paul, and who undoubtedly caught the passion of his life, could leave him in the end. However, the mystery of the whole matter is that anyone of us can gradually slip out of the center of things and get lost along the way.

At certain points in the life of Demas, the wrong affections and companions and loyalties began to tug at him. Finally, he began to see the allurement, the enticement of another way of life more and more. Then he began to think of how difficult this traveling around with Paul was. There were constant threats and always the possibility of death. He perhaps began to imagine more and more the laughter and gaiety of friends he had left back in Thessalonica. So finally, he slipped quietly away. He had become a spiritual dropout.

None of us decides on a certain afternoon that he will quit the Christian cause and go off to peddle his papers elsewhere. It happens so smoothly and imperceptibly we hardly know it's going on. Our mind begins to wander. We begin to go to sleep when we pray. We begin to become critical of others. How unglamorous and dull and square the whole thing begins to look! And finally we no longer show up.

It hasn't been one great event that did it. It has been a whole series of circumstances that led to a certain kind of deadness so that we no longer care. This is what produces the desertion of a Demas, the treachery of a Judas, the denial of a Peter.

We need in the church more people of the kind who stay close to the fire, who go the second mile when they need to go only one, who live by the disciplines when everyone else doesn't care. It is not without reason that Jesus said, "For the gate is narrow and the way is hard that leads to life, and those who find it are few." The grace of God is a costly gift; we cannot receive it casually, flippantly, or superficially. It demands our obedience which becomes the road of joy, power, and life.

We can avoid being a dropout only by staying close to the teacher and learning the lessons that finally lead to our graduation.

22. THE KEY TO THE LAST ROOM

A KEY IS SUCH AN INSIGNIFICANT-LOOKING AFFAIR, YET IT HAS TRE-mendous power. A key can open the door to the place you call home, or to a safe deposit box, or to a prison. How amazing that near the end of the New Testament there is a picture of Christ standing at a door asking admittance! In the Revelation of St. John there are these words: "Behold, I stand at the door and knock; if any one hears my voice and opens the door, I will come in to him and eat with him, and he with me." Here is life's greatest guest, standing at the door of life. The only one who can open that door is the one at whose heart he stands. Now, it is an easy thing to say that I will let Christ into my life — which card do I sign? or whose hand do I shake? — as if this were all an easy-going trans-action. The fact is that the most crucial, exciting encounter of all life is when we meet Christ and give him the key to our lives.

However, let us take this a step further: There is not only a key to the front door, but many, many rooms within a house which can be unlocked only with keys. I can let a guest into my living room but refuse to let him into the den or kitchen because those are untidy, ill-kept rooms. So I can lock those doors. We can chat with our guests in the lovely setting of one area of the house but keep them out of the other areas. Similarly, there's a kind of easy-going, nice religion that would keep Christ in the living room. The crucial question is, however: Have I let Christ come into that room of my life where the work is done, into the kitchen or the den or the bedroom?

There is an old story which concerns one of God's great men in England. It seems that Dr. F. B. Meyer had a dream one night. Christ came to him in the dream and asked him for the keys to his life. Dr. Meyer said he reached down and took the key chain off his belt and handed it to Christ. The Lord looked at the keys carefully, then asked Meyer, "Are these all the keys?" The good doctor gave the answer, "No, I have only one small key left to a very tiny room. Surely you wouldn't want that key?" With this Christ handed the keys back saying, "No, I must have *all* the keys or none of them at all." Dr. Meyer says he awakened from his troubled sleep with hot tears coursing down his cheeks. He then knelt by his bed and surrendered his life to his Lord in that hour. The fact is that he had carried a secret envy of a more successful pastor in his heart. From that hour when Dr. Meyer gave Christ *all* the keys to his life, there came a new power in his life.

This is a simple story that speaks to each of us. It is fine to allow Christ to come in where we put the nice furniture, but have we allowed him into the rooms where decisions are made, where we entertain our friends, where we have our secret thoughts, and where our checks are written? If he has never gotten into those rooms, what do we mean when we say that Jesus is the Lord of our lives? So it is, in the Revelation of St. John, that Christ stands with a nail-scarred hand, knocking at the door of a man's life. That man is free to reject or to answer his knock. His response must be his total surrender or it is not valid. Christ is eager to live in those areas where man has shut him out—in family life, in business, in man's approach to his neighbor, in his social life, in his loving, and, finally, in his dying.

Will you notice that, when we surrender, then we sup with our Lord? He joins us at dinner and there is joy at that banquet. My dear man, does Christ have the key to the last room in your life?

23. GETTING INTO THE DEEP

THIS SPRING OUR OLDEST SON AND I BUILT A SAILBOAT. THIS MAY NOT seem like much of a task to you; but, even with a kit, it was one of the major accomplishments of my life. The two of us had a great time getting the job done because we agreed that we would work only when both of us could be there. So finally after the two months of gluing and nailing, sanding and varnishing during every spare minute, our sailboat was finished. Then came the day of launching. To our amazement not only did our boat float, it was water tight. I assure you that this was a moment of great triumph.

But then came the task of learning to sail. We had read no books on the subject. All we had was a love for the water. Within a week we capsized enough times so that I was black and blue in many strange places and even had difficulty walking. As a matter of fact, one day two well-meaning fellows in a powerboat tried to rescue me. Imagine a sailboat being towed in by a motorboat! I declined their kindness and finally struggled home. But little by little we began to get the hang of it, and in those moments when we really sailed, I forgot all about those capsizing experiences. There was the sound of the wind in the sail and the cut of the prow in the water. I knew then that sailing had captured my heart.

Among the many things sailing has taught me, one of the most important is the adventure of getting out of the harbor into the deep where the wind and the waves wait for the sailboat. There is no sailing as long as one hugs the shore or stays tied to the buoy. One has to move out of quiet waters into the wind and the waves. This is where the mysterious power called the wind can move the boat and where the thrill of sailing comes.

Do you remember Jesus telling his disciples to launch out into the deep? They had tried to fish in shallow waters, but this was not good enough. Such is the way it is with sailing; there is no real sailing in the shallows. Here is a parable of life. For those of us who stay near home and never leave Mama's apron strings, there never comes the adventure of having fought the battles alone in becoming a real person. It is when we burn the bridges behind us and enter new experiences that life takes on rich meaning.

This is true of schooling. If our children were never allowed to cross the streets or to face the possibilities of being hurt on the playground, they would never learn their ABC's. This also is true of marriage. This high calling asks of us a willingness to give up the old for the new. Remember the words, "Therefore a man shall leave his father and mother and be joined to his wife, and the two shall become one."

Ah, there is danger in that, but there is also amazing possibility in it, and what is true of marriage is even more true of religion. As long as we try to live by little ideas which we can grasp concerning God and man, we will have a nice safe unexciting experience. But when we move out into the vast stretches of an eternal God, who invites us to better lives on his amazing promises at high risk, then we begin to sail. This is the deep. Think of how many of us have never grasped the wonder of obeying the word of Christ. We have lived by little moralisms wearing ourselves out trying to watch our P's and Q's. Beyond all this is the joy of surrendering to a higher will and power. Then we become channels for God's grace, not our own. This is the deep where we catch the wind and begin to have the thrill of sailing. It seems to me that what Christ is trying to do for most of us is to beckon us, call us, nudge us beyond quiet waters to the place where there are wind and waves. How we need to leave the shore and brave another cruise!

> I feel the winds of God today;
>   Today my sail I lift,
> Though heavy oft with drenching spray,
>   And torn with many a rift.
> If hope but light the water's crest,
>   And Christ my bark will use;
> I'll seek the seas at his behest,
>   And brave another cruise.[1]

[1] Jessie Adams. Used by permission of the Trustees of the Fellowship Hymn Book.

24. REJECTING THE RIGHT INVITATION

IT IS AMAZING HOW MANY TIMES JESUS TALKED ABOUT PEOPLE BEING invited to great, joyful affairs. These were never drab, colorless, innocuous affairs. They were always weddings, feasts, banquets, occasions where there was music and laughter and dancing. The invitation of Christ is always to abundant life, to freedom and joy, to the wonder of a great new adventure — for the kingdom of God is a life of peace, love, and joy.

It is strange, then, that so often Jesus spoke of men rejecting invitations to these dinners or wedding feasts. In the Gospel of Luke, he tells of a king who sent out his servants with invitations to a banquet. These servants came back with peculiar answers. One man could not come because he had bought a field; another begged off because he had secured five yoke of oxen; and a third even asked to be excused because he had married a wife. These were strange, almost insulting, answers to a great invitation. It was then that this king commanded his servants to go out into the streets and alleys to bring in the poor, the crippled, and the blind. Can you imagine the amazed reaction of bums and tramps living in squalor and in need when that kind of invitation came to them? These were the ones who became the honored guests at the great banquet. As this incredible dinner got underway there must have been embarrassed, almost frightened, silence. Then the loving, congenial host put everyone at ease with the right word or a small joke spoken here or there until the banquet hall finally rang with laughter and much talk.

Now, life is a maze of conflicting invitations. There isn't a one of us who couldn't do ten more things on a given day than he has strength or time to accomplish. All the way from the great worthy causes — the PTA, the United Fund, or the church meeting — to paying off social debts, they come. The question then is which invitations will I accept and which will I reject. And, here is where most of us lack a sense of priorities, a capacity for right choices. So for many of us life becomes like a squirrel cage or a merry-go-round. The helter-skelter events of a given day push us all over the place until we are drained of all creative energies, and we can't seem to get off the merry-go-round. The sad commentary on modern life is the number of talented, strong people who are giving their energies to little, secondary affairs. We beat our brains out trying to keep up with somebody else, or worrying about what "they" will say, or trying to satisfy ourselves on the fleeting, momentary things of life. In so doing we have settled for the field or the oxen or the marriage — and turned down the great invitation! We end up accepting the wrong invitations. It is one of the great paradoxes of life that people who have many things find it terribly difficult to accept the possibility of God's kingdom. So we miss the banquet, the abundant life of Christ, and settle for the lesser, and the fleeting.

How amazing it is that this great invitation of Christ's which could be limited to a few chosen people who are "in" has been opened to all of us! The good news is that we are invited. The door of God's grace is thrown wide open and the invitation has come by special messenger to our homes. We may say, "I am not good enough to go to this feast," or we may use the favorite argument that our clothes are not suitable. It may be that we are not certain how to act in the master's palace. None of this makes any difference. The message comes to those who are on the back streets, to those who live in little, dirty places, as well as to those who live in the fine houses.

None of us will ever know the wonder of the brightly lighted banquet hall, the goodness of the food, and the joy of being a part of this amazing fellowship unless he lays aside the excuses and dares to accept the single invitation sent by Christ.

Thomas Kilgore, Jr. . . . *is pastor of the Second Baptist Church in Los Angeles. He is also on the Board of Directors of the Church Federation of Los Angeles, a member of the Religious Witness Committee, chairman of the Civic Committee of Los Angeles, and director of the Western Bureau of the Southern Christian Leadership Conference. Dr. Kilgore has appeared as a guest speaker for various service clubs and other civic organizations and has participated in the Consultation on Continuing Education for the Ministry at Andover Newton Theological School.*

25. BRIDGING THE CHASMS

LIFE IS LIKE A DRAMA, WHERE EACH OF US PLAYS A PART AND THEN moves off the stage. For most of us our parts are a curious mixture of comedy, fantasy, tragedy, and pantomime. But life as a drama is much more important than Shakespeare's *Macbeth* summarized it in that fearful moment: "Out, out, brief candle, life's but a walking shadow, a poor player that struts and frets his hour upon the stage and then is heard no more: it is a tale told by an idiot, full of sound and fury, signifying nothing."

In the sixteenth chapter of St. Luke, where he tells the parable of the rich man and the beggar, Jesus puts life in a different kind of dramatic setting — a setting that is truer to life as we see it. This parable is a drama brought close to each of us, a drama in which we are one with the actors. Jesus was surrounded with certain tragic and destructive disorders in the social, economic, political, and religious life of his day — ever-present chasms that kept God's children from loving one another.

The basic story is simple, yet profound — so very suggestive of what can happen in a society of privilege and wealth. Luxury can become a powerful sedative. So often it can cushion the pricks of moral consciousness. It can isolate us from the rawness of life. It can produce moral and spiritual insensitivity.

Dives lived in luxury; Lazarus was poor and sick. At Dives' gate Lazarus longed for food, but none was given. The dogs were more compassionate than Dives. As the story unfolds, both men died. Dives went to hell, the unseen world depicting the whole torment, and Lazarus went to heaven, Abraham's bosom. Dives wanted Lazarus to give him a drink of water, but Abraham asserted that it could not be done, for an impossible gulf separated them.

Have you ever thought of the gulfs that separate God's children? There are national gulfs, racial gulfs, economic gulfs, class gulfs, and religious gulfs. Wherever these distinctions have led us to deny, hate, fail to see, or be unbrotherly to any of God's children, they have become dangerous chasms that should be bridged. We have chasms because we do not see one another. All the valid arguments for the destruction of segregation and for racial inclusiveness, whether in the church, school, or community, are based on the premise that in faith we must see one another in order to love and appreciate one another. Dives did not see Lazarus. It is impossible to love your fellowman if you do not see him as your fellowman. So often are we made aware of a tragic blindness in our country and world today! Jesus exposed this blindness as he spoke from the cross, "Father, forgive them; for they know not what they do."

The Good Samaritan was able and willing to help the fallen man because he was able to see him. Blind casualness makes us accept, without testing, too many conventional concepts, too many stereotypes. I think artist Dore was wrong when he portrayed Dives' servants driving Lazarus away from the gate with whips. Oh no, Dives was not that kind of rich man; *he just didn't see Lazarus.* He didn't see a lonely man, a man in dire poverty, a fellow son of God. Dives is a forerunner of a sizable segment of nominal Christians who accept segregation, discrimination, economic deprivation, and educational inequality of fellow human beings, without a word or act of protest. They are not mean; they just don't see. There's only one antidote to this blindness, only one that can bridge the chasms; it is love. This love is part of the hope we have in Jesus Christ. The height, depth, and width of the chasms have been determined by life's great chasm-digger: sin. But Christian faith tells us that sin has been conquered. Let us proclaim to the world that deliverance has come, the chasm has been bridged. Let us tell them to open their eyes, and in their view they will see their fellowman and, beyond him, God.

26. WINDOWS OF THE SOUL

THE PURPOSES OF A WINDOW ARE TO PROVIDE PLENTY OF LIGHT FOR A room that would otherwise be dark, and ventilation for a room that would be stuffy. The window also serves as a vantage point from which one may view and assess the scenery outside. These physical and practical purposes of a window suggest to us a symbol that has deep spiritual overtones. Man in his very nature lives often in the dark. His soul so often needs light. The inconsequential trivialities of life leave us like a stuffy, closed room, and we need to be ventilated. Our views are cut short by life's paradoxes and problems, and we need to find some point from which we can get a long and fresh view of life. Therefore, let us say that we need *"windows* of the soul."

Suffice it to say that we all have "soul windows" of one size or another, and we know their potentials. But, windows *get dirty* and must be washed and cleaned ever so often. Smoke and soot in the city, dust in the country, and cooking fumes all over have a tendency to cover windows and distort vision. To what extent have you permitted the smoke of disinterest, the soot of carelessness, the dust of selfishness, and the fumes of doubt to cover your window? A careful personal analysis of most of our lives would reveal that much window-cleaning is needed. As the poet Thomas Ken once wrote:

> Awake, my soul, and with the sun
> Thy daily stage of duty run;
> Shake off dull sloth, and joyful rise
> To pay the morning sacrifice.

When the windows of our soul are clear and open, we can see and feel and be illumined. Values fall in the right place when we are illumined. Recently, in a classroom in our city, a little boy in the fourth grade was telling his teacher and fellow-classmates what he did over the weekend. In a rather matter-of-fact way he said, "When my friends and I were on the way to steal some fruit. . . ." A statement like that by a fourth-grader tells us that his generation is in great danger. It says that corruption is so apparent in all areas of our society that many of our youth have no sense of shame, no scale of values. Those of us who have reasonably clear windows must help to restore some moral rootage in our society. In no uncertain fashion, we must know the value of storing up treasures for ourselves in heaven. We must emphasize the fact that faith is more important than functions, love is far superior to lust, morality is more valuable than money, and stewardship is more to be desired than social standing.

Christianity enjoins all true believers to a singleness of purpose. This singleness of purpose does not strip one of his freedom. Rather, it helps him to clear away all pseudo-freedoms that would cripple and dwarf him. When Jesus spoke of the body, he was saying that if the eye is open and generous, then it illuminates all the body. But, if it is half-closed and selfish, the body then is darkened. Here is an area which could stand much improvement.

Blind nationalism in this country and in many of the emerging nations of Africa and Asia strongly suggests to us that we need to open some eyes. It suggests that we need many more generous eyes; for where the eye is generous, the whole body is illumined.

There is still, however, a type of window that we have not discussed, namely, the stained-glass window. Some of the world's greatest art has been found in these windows in churches, cathedrals, and monasteries around the world. Here the purpose of the window is to inspire, to preserve the history of the church, to propagate the faith, and to aid in worship. But stained-glass windows do not automatically perform these and other religious functions. They are symbols of the reality that exists in the church fellowship. If the church is true to her mission, they have meaning. If the church is bound by tradition, customs, and community mores, they have a hollow and empty meaning.

In 1963, I saw the bombed-out Sixteenth Street Baptist Church in Birmingham, Alabama. I saw the window where the image of the face of Christ had been blown away. This reflection ran through my mind as I stood there: "How many images of Christ in windows around the world really and truly represent the indwelling of Christ in the church?"

27. THE ANSWER TO FAILURE

FAILURE IS HARD TO TAKE. EACH TIME ONE FAILS, HE HAS A FEELING of great inadequacy. When one is in the midst of failure, he has a strong feeling that he is in a great glass house and that all the world is looking on derisively. Failure is hard and depressing.

But, when one seriously looks at failure, he understands that it is in reality a vital part of human existence. All men have failed and fallen short. Perfection is found in God alone. When we view failure in this manner, we avoid two major pitfalls; namely, we do not despair and die away when we fail, and we are charitable and understanding toward our fellowmen when *they* fail. When I was a boy, I learned well the adage: "If at first you don't succeed; try, try again." This seems to be the universal answer to failure.

The annals of Old Testament history are filled with stories of failure followed by success. A classic among these is the story of the Exodus. Through ten plagues that Egypt experienced, the children of Israel were held fast in bondage, but under the leadership of Moses they kept trying. As they meandered through the wilderness, they gave up more than once. They conceded failure over and over, but Moses kept calling to them to try again. Their miraculous escape from the Egyptians into the Sinai desert was made possible because they had enough faith in Moses and in God to try again.

Our Pilgrim fathers and the early colonists in this country established a new nation because they would not give up. When over half of the Massachusetts Bay colonists died after the first winter in a new land, the rest did not give up. They had failed; but from failure they planted new crops and then waited on God. At harvest time that year, their faith was vindicated and they held America's first Thanksgiving Day service.

Abraham Lincoln, Frederick Douglass, William Lloyd Garrison, and others who believed that chattel slavery was wrong, experienced one failure after another, but they kept trying. And, though the cost of the abolition of slavery in our country was great and an awful Civil War had to be fought, this sadistic and demoralizing economic and social system was brought to an end.

Countless have been the failures in our developing and expanding economy. It is said that Thomas Edison challenged a young scientist, who had failed on an experiment 999 times, to try again; whereupon he did and succeeded. George Washington Carver failed many times before he discovered the almost unlimited commercial values of the peanut and the sweet potato. With these discoveries he revolutionized the South's farm economy.

In the final analysis, failure is a challenge to find the unlimited possibilities which lie about us. Failure says to us that there are other avenues that we have not traversed; there is other soil that has not yet been cultivated; there are other bejeweled mines that are still unexcavated; and there is limitless space still to be conquered.

As we look at our common failures, may we have the faith of a newspaper editor of a Chicago daily, who wrote these words in an editorial after the great Chicago fire in 1889: "We shall rise from these ashes and build a great city."

If you know failure today, don't be a cynic. Don't blame life for cheating you, or accuse it of being unfair to you. Look up! Reach for the hand of God. Faith in him is the answer to failure.

28. THE BROKEN PIECES

A FEW SUMMERS AGO A FRIEND OF MINE SPENT HIS VACATION ON AN island off the coast of Maine. Among the people he met was a young school teacher who was vacationing there, and who had a deep interest in religious art. Here is the account of the encounter between my friend and the teacher-artist, as my friend related it to me.

This particular Maine island has for years served as a base for lobster fishermen. During the off-season, fishing nets are left floating in the water and are buoyed by bottles tied to the nets. Some of the bottles were beer bottles, some were whiskey bottles, and some soft drink bottles. They were different shapes, sizes and colors. Often these floating bottles hit rocks and were broken, and the tides moved many of these broken pieces of glass ashore. The teacher-artist spent his vacation walking along the shore and gathering the broken pieces of glass. Back to a little studio in the rear of his cabin, he took these pieces. There, with his God-given ability, he turned these broken whiskey, beer, and soft drink bottles into stained-glass windows with religious motifs. My friend attested to the fact that these windows met the standard of real art, and portrayed a beauty that was authentic.

This story started a trend of thought in my mind. Little did the lobster fishermen think that these abandoned bottles of theirs would have any value beyond that of holding their nets afloat in the water; and little was the attention paid by the average vacationer to those broken pieces of glass lying on the shore. But, when they were discovered by the artist, they immediately had value.

Thomas Kilgore, Jr.

Human life is so much like these broken bottles, especially when we try one pursuit after another and find ourselves broken in the process. After an experience like this, we feel so often as if we are lying useless on life's shore, unnoticed and unwanted. Life is full of brokenness: Families are broken; communities are broken; cities are broken; and nations are broken. We spend billions of dollars every year trying to mend the brokenness of our day. Maybe our trouble is that we are not responding to the universal artist who is ready and willing to heal our brokenness and bind our life together in a whole that has purpose and meaning.

God has permitted men and women, boys and girls of various nationalities, races, creeds, and colors to be scattered upon the face of this earth. He has made possible all the elements needed for a universal window of understanding and brotherhood. We, in turn, are to respond to his sensitive hand and loving heart.

The questioner asks: "How can I respond?" The first step toward response is to know your isolation and loneliness when your life is not in harmony with the will of God. The second step is that of responding to the call and love of God as he bids all men to come to him and know life. He calls us each time we see a fellowman in need; each time we see an opportunity to spread love and goodwill. The third step is to answer the call of God and lose yourself in his service. He has promised that, if we lose our lives in his service, we will gain a life with greater meaning.

The challenge is yours. You may lie on life's shore in brokenness, or you may know wholeness and beauty by answering God's call.

69

29. THERE IS NO PLACE LIKE HOME

THE WORD "HOME" HAS MANY MEANINGS. WHEN ONE SAYS THAT HE is going home, the reference could mean anything from leaving work and returning to his family and place of personal abode to leaving China, Uganda, or London and returning to the United States. But those who have been influenced by the Judaeo-Christian heritage have long believed that the family home is intended to be a little corner in the kingdom of God. They have seen home as a place where mother, father, and children grow together into moral, ethical, and spiritual maturity.

In 1883 an American warship brought the remains of an American citizen back to our shores. This citizen had died 31 years earlier in Africa, and was buried in a lonely cemetery in Tunis. When his remains were returned, a funeral was held for him in the Nation's Capital. This final service was attended by the President, Vice-President, members of the Cabinet, Congressmen, Senators, Judges, and Officers of the Army and Navy. Tens of thousands of citizens, rich and poor, stood along Pennsylvania Avenue with bowed, uncovered heads and paid homage to this man. John Howard Payne was the citizen. He had written many plays; most of them had been forgotten. But one of them contained a little poem that most Americans remember. The chorus went like this:

Home, Home, sweet, sweet Home,
There's no place like Home!
There's no place like Home!

These lines touched the cord that vibrated in the hearts of millions of men and women the world over, and they still vibrate in many hearts today.

The home that is real is made up of persons — vital, communicat-

70

ing, growing persons. This means that there must constantly be an atmosphere of freedom. By freedom, I do not mean that each person will be permitted to do as he pleases, but rather that each person is free to do as he should. Freedom does not permit the growing child to smash the piano with a hammer, but it does give him the opportunity to learn to play the works of Bach and Chopin. The truly free person always acts under the enabling restraint of ideas and high aspirations.

Even though the apostle Paul was not a family man, and possibly did not as an adult maintain a home, he nevertheless gave some sound and basic teaching regarding family life and home life: "Children, obey your parents in the Lord, for this is right." This admonition is not advice for a bygone day; it is as relevant and as valid for children and young people now as it was in Paul's day. The sophistication and "hepness" of our day must in no way do away with good manners, the spirit of obedience, and the virtue of respect. If the freedom of our day does not presuppose a strong sense of responsibility, then we are in for long days and dark nights of trouble and despair.

"Fathers, do not provoke your children to anger, but bring them up in the discipline and instruction of the Lord." Modern psychology and psychiatry were unknown in Paul's day, but his counsel to parents cannot be improved upon by any of our modern methods. Things and gadgets are never good substitutes for love, understanding, and basic family nurture.

No, there is no place like home — when that home is blessed by a mother who loves and understands, a father who provides and cares, and children who respond in obedience and respect. When love dominates the home, God is there and he becomes the unseen but known presence in the family circle.

71

30. MEANINGFUL DIRECTIONS

NOT EVERYONE CAN GIVE DIRECTIONS CLEARLY. SOME PEOPLE ARE AS honest as a citizen in one of our great cities was when he replied to a tourist who was lost, "If I were you, I wouldn't try to reach that hotel from this point." Many others are not quite so honest, and they confuse travelers and lost persons many, many times.

The import of this brief message grows out of an experience I had several years ago. I was driving along on a state highway in the mountains of western North Carolina on a beautiful summer day, looking for an estate. Suddenly I felt that I needed information, and at that moment I beheld a service station, deserted except for an elderly lady who seemed to have seen many summers and winters come and go in those lovely mountains. Although disappointed that I did not stop to purchase gasoline, she was most cordial in her answers when I inquired for the exact location of the estate. This was her answer: "Drive on down this road, and don't turn at the first road you see on the right, but turn at the second road on the right. Now, as you drive out that road, it will be narrow and it will be dark. It will look like you ain't goin' to git there, but if you keep driving, you'll git there."

I was so fascinated by these directions that I remembered them well and followed them exactly. As I turned off on the second road to the right, I found it to be narrow and a bit rough. And as I drove along, the mountain flora and fauna seemed to close in on me. Soon the mountain ivy, mountain laurel, the rhododendron and

72

Thomas Kilgore, Jr.

other plants which grow so prolifically in that country formed an arch over the road and virtually turned it into a tunnel. At one point the darkness caused by the thick growth made it necessary for me to turn on the headlights of my car. Then the words came through clearly, "It'll look like you ain't goin' to git there." So I kept driving.

Almost as suddenly as I had spotted the lady who gave me the directions by the side of the road, the mountain growth seemed to fade away, and I found myself in a driveway leading to a majestic mansion built at the foot of the mountain. There I saw a beautiful terraced lawn, fruit trees, and lovely shrubbery. Inside the mansion I found welcome, warmth, and friendship. A good direction had paid off.

Shouldn't we all keep asking for proper directions in life? Don't all of us get lost at times? The candid answer is, "Yes." And, life with its strangeness and mystery gives to us the answers and directions from the most unexpected sources. A long time ago we were told by him whose directions are always right, "I am the way, and the truth, and the life." Our present age needs to listen to this simple, but profound, direction and then follow without faltering. If you do this, you will also hear him say above all the rough roads, dark tunnels, perils, and problems of this life, "In my Father's house are many rooms; if it were not so, would I have told you that I go to prepare a place for you?"

73

31. FAITH'S VENTURE

THE COMFORTS OF OUR MATERIAL ABUNDANCE HAVE MADE IT IMPERA-tive for us constantly to check our faith. The danger of losing sight of the fact that life is at all times a venture of faith is ever apparent. There are serious signs all about us that indicate a falling away from positive, daring living. Now, this doesn't mean that there is not a lot of daring living. The problem is that there is too much of the wrong kind — purposeless, daring living. May we never forget that the days of pioneers are not over and that the challenges of faith have not ended!

Years ago there was an old skipper who had charge of a Coast Guard Station on the rocky coast of Maine. On a bleak stormy night an S.O.S. call came to him. The call reported a wrecked ship that was sinking fast. The old captain had a new crew and he barked to them, "Launch the boat." One of his neophyte seamen paled with fear and stammered, "We are not going out on a night like this, are we? Why, we'll never get back." The old captain lifted himself to full stature, his broad shoulders expanding and his eyes flashing with courage. He looked the new, fearful crew-man straight in the eye and repeated his command: "Launch the boat. We have to go out, but we don't have to come back." This is always the stern imperative of faith's venture.

In an age of extreme rationalism and doubt, in a day in which such strong emphasis is placed upon scientific verification, it is well to remember that great ventures of faith have brought us where we

74

Thomas Kilgore, Jr.

are today. The discovery of our continent in the latter part of the fifteenth century was the result of a venture of faith. The many Spanish and African explorers who came to these lands in the fifteenth and sixteenth centuries were men of great faith. Our Pilgrim fathers left the shores of England and Europe, sailed the vast expanse of the Atlantic, landed at Plymouth Rock, and established themselves in the new land at a great sacrifice of life — all because they wanted religious freedom and because their faith was undaunted. The American dream is continuously unfolding as the "land of the free and home of the brave," because her citizens who represent various continents, nations, and cultures continue to have faith in a nation founded upon democratic principles.

Faith makes possible the seemingly impossible. Our Lord stood on a shore one morning after some of his disciples had fished all night, and calmly asked them, "Children, have you any fish?" Their answer was, "No." He said to them, "Cast the net on the right side of the boat." This they did and brought up an abundance of fish. Now, they had been fishing in this same area all night, and had caught nothing. What made the difference? These were experienced fishermen. They knew the waters. What made the difference? Was it a miracle? No! It was faith. Every venture of faith has its own rewards. Sometimes they are material, sometimes spiritual, and sometimes they are rewards of suffering. But such suffering brings wholeness. Don't fear the venture of faith!

32. THE IMPORTANCE OF SMALL THINGS

WHILE ON A TOUR OF JAPAN SEVERAL YEARS AGO, THE FATHER, AND only close relative, of our tour leader died in New England. Resigned to the impossibility of returning to the States for a service, he went with us the next day from Tokyo for a day's visit to the beautiful little resort city of Nikko. When we arrived at our hotel our guide, Mr. Shimizo, spoke to me as the temporary tour leader and said that he had arranged with the hotel to provide a special room for us with appropriate chairs, tables, and candles, so that we could "worship" the dead father of our tour leader. Even though his concept of honoring the dead was more Shinto than Christian, he, nevertheless, performed a small act of love and kindness that helped greatly to lift the burden of our leader.

What a wonderful world this would be if many more of us would give attention to small acts of love, kindness, and helpfulness. I know that this is easy to say, and difficult to do in a world that majors in *bigness*. But there is great danger that bigness may be unreal and hollow, if we do not understand the importance of small things. Many people are afflicted with the fatal attitude that says, "This little that I have is nothing. Why should I bother?" One should never permit this age of the "cult of bigness" to blind him to the intrinsic worth of his God-given possessions. The old adage, "Great oaks from little acorns grow," has not lost any of its meaning. And we should never forget that the mighty Mississippi, which empties into the Gulf of Mexico, begins as a small stream in northern Minnesota.

It was only a small jar of precious ointment that Mary used to anoint the feet of Jesus, but her tribute was an act of love which has been remembered for two thousand years. The boy in the multitude had only two fish and five barley cakes, but he freely gave them to Jesus, and one of the great miracles of the New Testament came to pass. David had only a sling and five smooth stones, but his faith in God and his desire for freedom put to use small things that ultimately toppled a large enemy.

The parable of the talents says to us clearly and distinctly that he who does well the small jobs at his hand always has greater ones waiting. Don't ever be so possessed with the big job, the great promotion, the distinct honor, and the high place that you overlook the small job and the everyday acts of kindness and goodness. Broadway producer Eddie Dowling said that when he interviews actors and actresses for roles in his plays, he asks them to say only two lines — "I love you" and "I believe in God." If they can read those two lines well, they can play any role.

"Silly Joe" was known by all the townspeople of a small Long Island village. Joe was retarded. He made no progress in school. But he grew into manhood in his community, and he made at least two real contributions. When he walked down the street, he smiled cheerfully and spoke to everyone he met. This often brought cheer to the housewife as she rushed to do her shopping, or to the stuffy businessman who had been through a rough business deal. Joe's second contribution was that he kept the lawn of his church beautifully groomed. His gifts were small, but, oh, how important! Are you doing as much with your gifts?

33. DO WE WANT PEACE?

Do you really want peace? If your answer is "yes," then do something about it! So many of us talk about peace as if it were a state of quiet and blissful contentment, far removed from the problems and perplexities of rugged daily living — or as if it were sort of a vacuum of tranquility between bloody, armed clashes on one side and social-revolution impasses on the other. It is little wonder that we continue to cry "Peace, Peace," and still there is no peace.

We live in a world of troubled hearts. There is such a compilation of national, state, and individual guilt complexes that our guilt, anxiety, and fear in all too many instances explode in violence, social disruption, and destruction. In reality this should be our hour of happiness. Our expectations and projections should be higher than ever.

Archaeologists tell us that they will discover a new geography deep below the surface of the earth which will reveal flower-enclosed playgrounds for children, rich treasuries, and descriptions of antiquities hidden in lost cities. Basic research will soon make possible, by applied technology, millions of work opportunities high in the sky and deep down on the ocean floor. Automation, with its frightening possibilities, is not really rushing us to a quick end of the world. It is really reminding us that progress for mankind is the will of God. But the great heritages of man that are needed to be handed down from generation to generation are not properly transmitted, because we miss out so completely on a fundamental lesson: "Peace I leave with you; my peace I give to you; not as the world gives, give I to you."

We have taught ourselves such bad lessons, and chief among these is the one of absolute ownership of certain portions of the earth. If Judaeo-Christian teachings make anything plain, they clearly state that "the earth is the Lord's, and the fulness thereof"; that God owns the earth and we possess it for a time as trustees. When this simple lesson is learned, we will have made a great step toward peace.

Just as God is creator and owner, he is also father. This makes all human beings his children. Though we come before God and our fellowmen in many colors, sizes, temperaments, cultures, and intellects, we are all his children — and each one is precious in his sight. If, then, we are all his children, we are all brothers and sisters; if brothers and sisters, then we are in one family. Our enemy, therefore, becomes not one another, but the common enemy of the family. If we want peace, let us turn to fight the enemies of God's children — such enemies as poverty, disease, exploitation, segregation, discrimination, and racism. To many of us, this confrontation would create some strange comrades in arms, but to all of us, it would ultimately bring peace.

34. REDISCOVERING KINDNESS

THERE IS A SHINING VIRTUE THAT IS ALL TOO OFTEN NEGLECTED, AND all too often neglected by good people. This virtue is kindness. As St. Paul makes a plea for the practice of the virtue of kindness, he seems to suggest that we think of ourselves as belonging to a society which prevents cruelty to our fellowmen.

Phillips' translation of Paul's words to the Ephesians suggests that kindness should be shown in thought, speech, and action. "Let there be no more resentment, no more anger or temper, no more violent self-assertiveness, no more slander, and no more malicious remarks. Be kind to each other, be understanding. Be as ready to forgive others as God for Christ's sake has forgiven you." In our present language the words "kind" and "mankind" are closely related. In its root meaning, a kind person is a "kinned" person — one who acknowledges relationship, debt, and tie. Kindness, then, is more than inspired amiability that helps one to be regarded as a nice person. Kindness is love expressed powerfully and intelligently.

The kind person sets about to make goodness attractive. The story is told about two women who were talking about a third woman. As they talked over the back fence, they fenced and hedged a bit — each withholding what she really thought about the other woman. Finally, one said, "Well, she is a good woman, anyhow." Whereupon the other answered, "Well, I don't like her either." This may be an amusing little story, but it is tragic in that it points up the fact that goodness is so often unattractive.

Kindness is the art of making our goodness attractive. A little girl, after her first Sunday in church school and after an encounter with a very firm and austere teacher, said in her prayer that night, "Dear God, make all the bad people good; and please make all the good people nice." This was a real prayer. Let us never forget that sourness is not a badge of saintliness; nor is gloominess a proof of piety. Make sure that you do not possess a hard core. A soft and warm heart is always preferable to one that is righteous but forbidding. Kindness is the antidote to moral insensitivity and hard-heartedness.

If you would be kind, bring appreciation to others, cultivate the understanding heart, and add a little brightness to each person you meet, then it is likely you will have the blessings expressed in the following old Irish poem:

> The blessings of blessings for him
> That has always time to be kind.
> A blessing running before,
> A blessing trotting behind;
> An angel caring for his house
> To drive away every sorrow.
> Good luck at his heels today,
> Good luck on his path tomorrow:
> A place for him up in heaven
> And St. Peter there at the gate
> With the kindly welcome word,
> And himself not bid to wait:
> For I'm thinking the Saint will say,
> "Come in here out of the *wind,*
> It's not so often I see
> A man that has time to be *kind.*" [1]

[1] Author unknown.

35. A CHRISTMAS MESSAGE

THE EVENT WHICH GAVE US CHRISTMAS BEGAN WITH A SONG, AND IN the growth of Christianity, singing has been an important medium and a unique expression of faith. In this manner, Christmas is related to many other great historical events that have used poetry and music to express their inner meanings, their truest desires and sentiments. Early Americans sang lustily their ballads, the soldiers of our nation have marched proudly to the music of the military bands, the Negro American expressed his soul's desire in the great spirituals, and the celebration of Christmas is never complete without the singing of carols and all of the other great Christmas music that is the spiritual continuation of the angelic hymn, "Glory to God in the highest, and on earth peace among men with whom he is pleased!"

Our souls can be refreshed by listening to great Christmas music. It can be a great antidote in this crassly materialistic age. A hundred years ago Emerson said, "Things are in the saddle and riding mankind." The challenge before us today is to use the things which God has permitted us to possess to his glory and honor. The accretions of Christmas that have snowballed through the centuries — leaves, tinsel, trees, holly wreaths, mistletoe, plum pudding, colored lights, gifts, cards, and bills — though bulky, need not detract from the beauty and real meaning of Christmas. In faith we believe that God is expressing his nearness to us by allowing us to be the stewards of so many things. In turn we express our appreciation to him by sharing with others our abundance. The music of Christmas and the sharing of our abundance and love for God and for one another puts us in the frame of mind and spirit to see the revelation of true worth and power.

Christmas began in a world of turmoil. Caesar Augustus was emperor of Rome whose dominions extended over all the Mediterranean, north to Britain, and eastward to Asia. It was said that, when the Roman legions and engineers moved in and conquered new cities and territories, they found them brick and left them marble. The rule of Caesar Augustus was a rule of wealth, power, and authority.

In a corner of a plain province of this vast empire, sometime between 6 and 3 B.C., a babe was born in a town named Bethlehem, to which Mary and Joseph had gone to be counted. He was born in a stable, and not in the inn — there was no room for him there. His birth gave us Christmas, and his life, death, and resurrection have given us a faith that has outlived the Roman Empire. In a sense, the influence of this babe dethroned the emperor and proclaimed a kingdom mightier than that of the Romans. It told of a world saved not by a man who tried to become God, but by God who became man.

No one needs to feel that God is far away. No amount of failure and hopelessness should dim anyone's desire to reach God and to communicate with him. He is not far away and he is not impersonal, not unreal. He is always very present and very near. The real essence of the spirit of Christmas affirms our faith in the nearness of God.

When Galileo was accused of moving God so far out into the outer space of the universe that men felt forsaken and grew discouraged, he made this thoughtful reply: "The sun, which has all these planets revolving around it and dependent upon it for orderly functions, can ripen a bunch of grapes as if it had nothing else in the world to do." These words are so well-spoken and so symbolic of the Christmas spirit that they help us to understand that in Christmas we add to our sense of God's majesty the knowledge of his tenderness.

When one reads Luke's beautiful and sensitive account of the birth of Jesus, he hears in the singing of the angels and sees in the action of the shepherds an adoration that is expressive of the kind of response that comes from experiencing the nearness of God.

36. ON TALKING TO ONE'S SELF

MOST OF US THINK PEOPLE ARE FUNNY OR PECULIAR WHEN THEY TALK to themselves. Think of the way you react when you meet someone on the street, or see someone in an automobile, talking to himself. We are amused at such antics; but, when we stop to think a bit, we discover that all of us talk to ourselves at one time or another and that what we say is quite important.

We live in a world in which we are greatly influenced by the words of others. Bitter and hateful words can do harm beyond measure, and words spoken rightly and kindly can do endless good. Someone has said that a word, fitly spoken, is like an apple of gold in a picture of silver. The powerful words of great personages in history have gripped man by his shoulders and awakened him. They have also broken the drought of the soul and set life flowing. It was Job's friends who said, "Your words have upheld him who was stumbling." We are therefore cautioned to be careful of what we say to others, for words have power to hurt or power to help, power to kill or to make alive.

Now, if what we say to each other is important, what we say to ourselves is even more important. In fact, that which you habitually say is YOU. Let me illustrate with three New Testament stories:

There was a wealthy farmer who was successful and upright, an honorable pillar of society. We don't know too much about his family or his background, but we know him by the way he talked to himself. He was fortunate enough to be in the position to reap a bumper crop. And, in that case, it seems as if he would have said, "God has been good. My workers have been faithful. I have more than I need, so I'll give to the poor." But he said, instead: "I will pull down my barns, and build larger ones; and there I will store my grains and my goods. And I will say to my soul, Soul, you have ample goods laid up for many years; take your ease, eat, drink, be merry." As he talked to himself, he revealed that he was a moral imbecile, and that he was completely bereft of appreciation for life's higher values.

There was a woman who talked to herself. Life for her had been hard. She came to the springtime of life with a shameful disease. She had to forfeit marriage and motherhood. She had some money, but spent it all trying to get well. She could have said, "I'll give up and die." But, she didn't. She reasoned, "I'm sick, but I am not dead," and faith told her that Jesus possessed healing for her. So she said to herself, "If I only touch his garment, I shall be made well." This is the kind of daring conversation each of us must carry on with ourselves. This is the way to keep hope alive. This is the way to lick doubts. This is the way to live.

The prodigal son talked to himself when he found that he was without money, friends, and dignity. He looked at his sordid surroundings and thought of the comforts of his home. Then he began a conversation with himself. Listen as he says, "I will arise and go to my father." He continued to talk of the comforts and the privileges of his home, and soon talked himself into the long journey back home. If you really know how to talk with yourself, your prologue soon turns into a dialogue with the one who is the way, the truth, and the life.

Lee Shane . . . *was for several years pastor of the National Baptist Memorial Church in Washington, D.C., which is affiliated with both the American and Southern Baptist Conventions and has a special witness in the Nation's Capital to the cherished principle of religious liberty. He also served as pastor of the Calvary Baptist Church in Charleston, West Virginia.*

Active in the field of broadcasting for many years, Dr. Shane has been chairman of the Radio and Television Committee of the Council of Churches in the National Capital Area, and was chairman of the Radio and Television Committee of the American Baptist Convention. He conducted an award-winning television program, "The Church's Big Story," for the West Virginia Council of Churches.

37. THOSE WONDERFUL O'S

JAMES THURBER WROTE SEVENTY-TWO PAGES OF DELIGHTFUL SATIRE denouncing the censorship of what people hate. He called it *The Wonderful O*.

It concerns a man named Littlejack, who had a ship; and another man called Mr. Black, who had a map. Mr. Black hated everything with the letter O in it. His hate of O was allegedly because his mother had become wedged in a porthole, and they couldn't pull her in, so they had to push her out.

Besides Mr. Black's repugnance for O's he had a lust for precious jewels. The map he had indicated that on an island called OOROO, admittedly a distasteful name to Mr. Black with all those O's, there was hidden a fortune in precious gems.

Black and Littlejack, upon arriving on the island with their unscrupulous crew, set about removing everything on the island with the letter O. The baker had no dough! The goldsmith had no gold! The tailor had no cloth! Everything with an O had to go!

But one day the islanders rebelled over losing all their O's and determined there were four words with an O that must never be lost. Three of them were hope, love, and valor. And the fourth word which "gleamed and glowed and glittered" was freedom.

Let me suggest some wonderful O's found in your Bible, which are worth holding on to. "To him that loves us and has loosed us from our sins by shedding his blood — he has made us a realm of priests for his God and Father — to him be glory and dominion for ever and ever" (Revelation 1:5-7, Moffatt).

Loves! Loosed! Blood! God! Glory! Dominion! All wonderful O's that set themselves to music, having the sound of a doxology. They "gleam and glow and glitter," these wonderful O's, and they must never be lost!

Lee Shane

There is only time to behold the wonder of one of these wonderful O's. *"Loosed* us from our sins." A figure, of course, of liberation. We have understood this to mean pardon for our transgressions; the demolition of the power of evil in our lives; the birth of a "new creature."

Being "loosed" from our sins is more than a pardon, it is more than the creation of a sinless wonder. Try, would you please, being a prisoner for a few seconds and maybe you can catch a hint of what this "loosing" means. You now are restricted by walls, held by chains, and you are aware of nothing so much as this imprisoning factor. You are prison-oriented! You are prison-directed! Prison-dominated! No factor in your life is so large in determining what you do as this prison.

Now, someone comes and "looses" you from that prison. It no longer dominates, it no longer directs your life. You gain a new orientation.

Sin is our prison. Sin is our human bondage, and we spend our lives sin-oriented, sin-directed, sin-dominated! We are conscious of and consumed by this major failure of our lives — this falling short of God's mark — and we desperately try to make up for this falling short by acts of goodness, acts of penance, thus relieving our guilt feelings. We hope to strike an over-payment of goodness and thus be acceptable to God.

But here comes God, who loves us. He comes to our prison and he "looses" us from our sins. Our inadequacies no longer are central in importance. Instead it is the adequacy of God and his love that is central.

Those wonderful O's — we must never let them go! He that "loves us and has loosed us from our sins. . . ."

38. BEWARE THE FIERCE LAMBS

I WOULD ARREST YOUR ATTENTION WITH SOME ODD WORDS THAT ARE found in the Book of Revelation. Here they are! "And the Lamb will conquer them, for he is Lord of lords and King of kings."

Honestly, now, have you been in the habit of associating a lamb with a Titan? A lamb in seven league boots is a bit out of character, don't you think? Yet, here is just such a lamb! "And the lamb will conquer them!"

This writer is dealing with the dimension of eternity and has resorted to deceptive symbol. All artists do this, of course. That is, they engage in a certain falsification in order more effectively to convey truth. We sometimes call this practice poetic license.

Anyway, this is what we have in Revelation. For there is no real lamb, no real beast, no real war. These are striking figures of something beyond themselves. This is hostility painted with bold, grotesque strokes. The malignant forces in the world are depicted as dramatically horrible as imagery can make them. And, the benevolent forces are depicted as meek and mild — like lambs ready for unprotested slaughter; no match whatsoever for the cruel beasts of the earth.

The author is describing a period when it seems that God has given up his office; closed shop; when the enemy of God is drunk now with "the blood of the saints." The final devastating blow against good is about to be delivered. Then suddenly, out of this hopelessness, there is a promise of a rescue: "And the Lamb will conquer them."

There you have the symbol. Now what is it all about? Well, it's about what is going on in history — about this frightening con-

90

tention between good and bad. It says that God has not abdicated, and although Evil does strut this hour on the stage, it shall soon "play its part and be heard of no more." The disciplined, the dedicated meek shall inherit the earth. The lamb, never figured to make devils tremble, will conquer.

This symbol says that the last word is not to be with violence or brutality. The final arbitrator in human affairs is not to be the bomb. Tears, death, suffering, and injustice will not cast their sorry spell indefinitely. The power of all these monsters is but for one hour, and then "the Lamb will conquer them."

All of this argues that the most desperate situations which you and I face are never a summons to despair, but to hope. We do live in a period when the moral tone of things is sagging very badly. Giant agonies beset this earth everywhere. The spiritual lamps are flickering feebly. The fierce beast stalks the earth and writes the headlines.

But this we have — the promise of rescue. "The Lamb will conquer!" Jesus Christ is that Lamb; Jesus Christ is the final arbitrator. His glory ascending like the dawn's banners! His power like the constraint of the tides gathering all things unto himself. His reconciliation, taking strangers and foreigners and making them fellow citizens in the household of God.

This world, I tell you, is stamped with that promise; its redemption guaranteed. There is no hope in anything before this, and there is no word more sure. Take it in your hands and hearts and put it against this night of Evil. . . . "And the Lamb will conquer them, for he is Lord of lords and King of kings."

39. DO-IT-YOURSELF ANNIHILATION

FIVE MINUTES OF THE LATEST NEWS WAS PASSED ON TO JESUS FOR his comment. Pilate, they said, had killed some Jews while they were worshiping in the Temple — mingling the worshipers' blood with the animals' which they were offering in sacrifice.

Jesus waved aside the political and theological implications of that brutal story: He ignored the haunting question of the innocent suffering. Instead, he sounded a warning: "Unless you repent, you will all likewise perish." What relevant words these are for our twentieth century! Repent, or perish!

Today's world is a kind of Leaning Tower of Pisa which threatens to come tumbling down. Many believe that a thermonuclear explosion will bring it down permanently. If some nervous finger gets to the atomic button, we are all in for annihilation!

Against this doomsday backdrop we need to measure these words of Jesus — "Unless you repent, you will all likewise perish." The deterrent to extinction is repentance.

We keep supposing that the finger that will push the button and release annihilation will be a military finger. Not necessarily so! Annihilation is more likely to be do-it-yourself! The fingers of 180 million Americans are my greatest worry.

Potentially, each one of us has a finger on that button. Every single act that any of us engage in, which has in it denial of moral and spiritual directives, is an act propelling us toward extinction. On the other hand, any act that shows repentance and acceptance of God's directives in social relationships is insurance against annihilation.

You may ask, "Why should I repent?" For one thing, there is this prevailing American heresy of considering God servant instead of sovereign. Our blasphemy is not that we use God's *name* in vain; it is that we use *God* — use him for our ends, use him for our purposes. We can't keep up this giving pious little nods to God on Sunday morning, and then go straight out Monday morning to be the most materialistic people on this earth. Continue this patronizing, and something is going to blow up. He who made us is not going to knuckle down and be our stooge. We had better repent of trying to make God into Mortimer Snerd, or get ready for the sad consequences.

Then there is something else calling for repentance; it is this widespread denial of our fellowmen as our brothers and loved of God. Divided cities today are the badge of our hostile nature. Walls and curtains emphasize our divisions of East from West, Free from Communist, Jew from Arab, Negro from White.

The Christian religion is dedicated to the removal of all walls, and calls the process reconciliation. In the context of the Christian church a "wall-less-ness" is to be demonstrated. This is why the repudiation of any believer in Jesus Christ because of gender, race, class, or background is a denial of the gospel and is the monstrous sin of our time because it defies the central affirmation of our faith, that in Christ the whole bundle of mankind is redeemed from alienation.

Unless the gospel can demonstrate its power to put down these deep hostilities which divide person from person, it just doesn't have much relevance to the very thing that's about to blow us off the map.

Unless we repent of denying our fellowman as brother, we "will all likewise perish"!

40. FUNERALS ARE NOT FINAL

JOB HAD HIS PROPERTY AND HIS FAMILY SWEPT AWAY FROM HIM SO suddenly that it takes your breath away just to read about it. Infectious disease puts a festering finger on his body, reduces him to around-the-clock-nursing of putrid sores. With no blessings to count, the poor man's mind is invaded by the death wish. In one of these wish-to-die moods Job asks an agelessly relevant question, "If a man die, shall he live again?"

I wonder why he put it in the subjunctive? "*If* a man die. . . ." Death is just not very "iffy." Getting into the obituary column is most certain. Every graveyard is mute evidence that death is real and death is earnest, and no one can put in for exemption. But the question is not about the probability of death, but the probability of life *after* death. Are funerals final?

One thing you observe about those days when Jesus lived: they were difficult days to have a successful funeral. One poor widow made it all the way to the gate of the burial-ground with the body of her only son; then Jesus came bursting on the scene. With a brief sentence and a touch, he broke up that sad procession and sent everyone back home.

Or when death came to that Bethany home, and Lazarus was bound in grave-clothes and buried, everybody was convinced that funeral was final. Four days later, Jesus came along to dispute their conviction. He cupped his hands before the grave and called Lazarus by name, and "the dead man came out." "Unbind him," Jesus said, "and let him go!"

Then one day death came and made its boldest move; it laid claim to Jesus himself. That day the sun veiled its face and the foundations of the earth trembled. While Pilate washed his hands of a sticky political situation, Nicodemus conducted a hasty funeral.

94

The disciples' shoulders stooped; they presented sad countenances everywhere, and some of them displayed shameful cowardice. Everything seemed determined to declare that this funeral for Jesus was final.

But God began writing an exciting postscript. An empty tomb! Discarded burial clothes! An angel taking the stone that had sealed the tomb and using it for a park bench! The announcement: Jesus you seek? He is not here among the dead, for he is alive! He is risen!

Now the sad countenance, the stooped shoulders, the shameful cowardice of those disciples is thrown aside; and, drunk with a new hope, they run to the four corners of the earth shouting: "Jesus Christ, raised from the dead hath abolished death and brought life and immortality to light. Because he lives, we too shall live!"

There is your answer, Job! And yours, too, if you are asking today: "If a man die, shall he live again?" Funerals are *not* final! Vacated graves, not vast plots of drying bones! Not weeping and mourning and dusty death, but whoever shall believe in Jesus Christ "should not perish but have eternal life."

Why not face your days as if this were true? Trust your loved ones to him. Keep coming back through every moment of doubt, every lonely moment of sorrow, to this faith that Jesus Christ does have the keys to unlock every tomb. Trust yourself to him in the faith that the dark portals of death are the doorway into a personal Easter — a corridor to the lasting city of God.

"If a man die, shall he live again?" Are funerals final?

Remember Jesus Christ, raised from the dead, "who abolished death and brought life and immortality to light through the gospel."

41. I WILL ARISE
AND GO TO MY MOTHER

HAS IT EVER STRUCK YOU THAT LUKE NEVER CONCERNS HIMSELF WITH the mother of the Prodigal? He felt he was dispensing all the important information necessary when he stated: "There was a *man* who had two sons." Here you have the most winsome family story in all the world, yet the mother of that family does not get a mention. When the bedraggled boy has his hour of moral renewal he says, "I will arise and go to my father." The ring, the robe, the shoes, the party, the forgiving; all are the father's doing!

Now this is no plea for "momism," but I would like to get in a word to and for the women of our world. I happen to believe that if we are ever going to find our way back to purposefulness, more women must put their strength into the situation.

Adlai Stevenson once told the girls at Smith College that their task was to keep Western man truly purposeful, that they were to develop in him that balanced tension of mind and spirit which can properly be called integrity. I will go right along with this world statesman in stressing this role for women.

You know, don't you, that we have now gained the dubious honor of spawning more prodigals than any previous generation in history. The specialists in the ills of society tell us why. They contend that bad boys and bad girls are the consequence of bad men and bad women. They say that a boy leaves his home to cut didoes in some far country because of something wrong in the home — the mother dominated, the father was a tyrant, the educational level was too low, the pay envelope too small. Anyway, they say, give a good home and you get good children!

Without denying that bad young people are sometimes the result

96

of bad homes, let's recognize that the home is not the only conditioning factor at work on the youth today. No home today is an isolated island, but is exposed to influences which contradict and countermand the values taught in the home. Luke's Prodigal has to go to his far country before he is exposed to corruption. Today our far country comes walking right into the living room. Every home is invaded by radio, television, magazines with subverting moral and spiritual values. Even a trip to the corner drug store for a soda exposes our youth to racks of erotic literature.

Most of this far country that insists on coming to us is man-directed. By and large, it is the male animal who has lost purpose and integrity. The evidence of this shows on the basketball courts, football fields, the board rooms of large corporations, in the legislative cloak rooms. Some of this corruption is low class and some of it is high class, some is by little-knowns and some is by well-knowns; still, it is the male animal who does it.

This is bad enough, but it is worse when the restorers of purpose are content to be receptors — beautifully dressed, beautifully coiffed, beautifully perfumed — just watching, tolerating, enduring this sorry race for goods and status.

With things getting morally out of hand, who is going to keep us purposeful and restore integrity if women become more and more blasé, failing to put their natural strength into this fight?

The Bible speaks of the virtuous woman saying, "Strength and dignity are her clothing." Remember that, will you, and if you have been chosen by God to be a woman, may you be moved to give the world your treasure.

42. THIS IS NOT MY FATHER'S WORLD

IF YOU HAVE HAD ANY EXPOSURE TO THE CHURCH, YOU SHOULD BE familiar with the hymn "This Is My Father's World." The song speaks of the rustling grass, the caroling birds, the rocks and trees, the skies and seas — all nature singing to God.

I pondered this anthem of nature to the Almighty while standing before the Library of Congress in the Nation's Capital. My eye was captivated by strange, tiny insulators strung with wire on all the window ledges and protrusions of that building. Those wires, winding over all the ledges, carried electric current, and were there to keep God's creation, birds, from despoiling man's creation, the building.

"This Is My Father's World"? Those charged ledges said to any black starling or pigeon taking rest from flight: This is *not* your Father's world.

As I contemplated this "cold war" between God's world and man's, another idea kept pulling at my sleeve — the big gap between *my* world and *my earthly father's* world. This is *not* the same old world, not *my father's* world! There is a sense in which the world remains constant . . . the same hungers, same pains, fears, and sins. There are a few changes in the actors from my father's world, but the same plot unfolds in every generation.

But, if my father could burst his grave clothes, he would hardly recognize this as the same place that he lived and loved in.

Rod Serling wrote a story about Flight 33 which was a 707 Boeing jet flying from London to Idlewild on a routine flight in June, 1961. The strange thing which happened was that Flight 33 broke the time barrier. When the plane got over Manhattan Island, the real estate was there, but no buildings and no people. The only thing visible was a giant dinosaur nibbling leaves off a tree, blinking huge puzzled eyes at what he assumed was a giant bird. That aircraft had gone back 5 million years in time, and there was no place in that world for a Boeing 707.

The story points up our dynamic, fluid world. It moves from dinosaurs to fan-jet aircraft, to space vehicles, to weekends on the moon.

Simon Peter once stood on a narrow street before a house with a large upper room where a strange wind had blown upon the occupants. He explained to the people that a new world was aborning in that wind. And he exhorted them to get out of the old world: Save yourselves from this crooked generation! Turn your back to the old! Be baptized into the new! This is not your father's world! Repent! Believe! Receive the Spirit of this new world!

Another man lay in the dust of a road at high noon. He discovered it was the dust of a different world – a world where the risen Christ turned up at every corner. And he kept saying from Damascus to Rome: Old things are gone! Behold all things are new, particularly the man that is in Christ Jesus.

This is not our father's world. It is a world in which revolution is in progress and giant agonies are being committed; a world of great achievements and mighty dreams.

Jesus Christ, back on a green mountain, later on a bleak hill, began these mighty dreams when he sought to make it plain that no man is beyond hope and no situation is beyond redemption.

It is very much a new world today, and you and I are going to have to understand, as did those of the New Testament, that this new world must be matched by new men.

99

43. A QUESTION FOR SIT-INNERS

IT HAS BEEN A WEARY FORTY YEARS SINCE THAT SLAVERY IN EGYPT; but by the grace of God and the patient persistence of Moses the Israelites are about to set foot on the Promised Land.

A military strategy is being devised to dislodge the present inhabitants. It is at this crucial point that a segment of the Israelites, for reasons of their own, feel no constraint to go any further. They say to Moses — "If we have found favor in your sight, let this land be given to your servants for possession; do not take us across the Jordan." This was a request to be counted out of the coming battles, and for the privilege of going about their own business.

Moses swings a sledge hammer down on that audacious proposal. His words erupt like hot lava against their dull conscience: "Shall your brethren go to war while you sit here?" Is this what you ask — to luxuriate in this fertile valley, indulging yourselves, while your brethren conquer the ground still held by the enemy? This you would do — sit here, while your brothers go to war?

The old prophet makes it plain that anyone who allows others to fight the battle for justice and opportunity, while they themselves engage in self-interest, is turning from God; and this is sin.

Just now I address that ancient question of Moses to you of the twentieth century: "Shall your brethren go to war while you sit here?" Those words have a bite in them for all the socially irresponsible and unconcerned, for all the comfortable people who have what they want and are content to sit and enjoy it while others are suffering for trying to win their inheritance.

Some of us have thought that if we kept the Ten Commandments we had pretty well qualified for God's approval. That is not so, not at all! Here is something not touched at all by the Ten Commandments — a turning away from social responsibility — and that too is sin. This brief message may not be enough, but I would convict you of this sin.

When any of us stand apart from the battles that are going on in this world, luxuriating while others go to these wars, this is the most ignominious and shameful iniquity of our time. He who seeks to exempt himself from the agonies of his brethren, refusing to get involved in the wars people are waging for an inheritance, is heading for a black night of the soul.

There is a new urgency for you to identify with the brethren in the church today, not merely in terms of your presence at worship come Sunday; but in joining these brethren as they contend with the modern Philistines.

Shame on you for disbarring yourself from the agonies of the earth; for this colossal indifference while your brethren are at war! You have, like the rich young ruler, kept the Ten Commandments from your youth up, but what about the area of social concern? Are you not, in your self interest, seriously offending here?

Oh the glory that might begin to dawn on this earth tomorrow if you would abandon your emancipation from responsibility, and join your brethren in the wars they are waging today for truth, justice, and righteousness in this earth.

Here is a text to haunt you, then, until your conscience is fully awake: "Shall your brethren go to war while you sit here?"

44. STOP THE WORLD: I WANT OFF!

HAVE YOU EVER GOTTEN INVOLVED IN SOMETHING AND WISHED YOU hadn't? My wife once got into a carnival contraption in which you were seldom right side up. Now, why anyone pays good money to enjoy these strange agonies, I could never quite understand. Anyway, not long after the ride was under way I heard a delirious outcry that would have done credit to the castle ghost. It was one of those hair-on-end screams that only a desperate woman could make.

This scream was provoked by the fact that this commercial torture chamber had stalled with the basket containing my wife at the very top. There she dangled, much too long for comfort, feet above head, and the head screaming, "Stop this thing! I want off!"

The Old Testament has a story about a man who got into something from which he wanted off. He came along in a time particularly out of joint. The dominant figure in his world was a woman. This woman was so implacable and deeply evil that, although three thousand years have passed since she lived, her very name is a byword for evil. The man was Elijah! The woman, Jezebel!

The major conflict between Elijah and Jezebel was over religion. They had different gods, and were both extraordinarily missionary-minded. They decided that they would resolve this conflict of their religion by a pragmatic demonstration. "Let that God be God," they said, "who can bring down fire from heaven."

It was an elaborate and exciting contest which went rather badly for Jezebel. Her priests could produce no fire from heaven despite all-day incantations and lacerating of themselves. On the other hand, Elijah spent a quiet moment on his knees in prayer and a bolt

102

of fire from the sky gave pretty convincing proof as to the power of his God.

Now, Jezebel, unhappy with the turn of events and a woman not easily put aside, vowed to kill Elijah, whereupon Elijah got a king-sized depression and ran away. When he stopped running, beneath a juniper tree, he screamed to God: "Stop the world: I want off!"

Elijah makes a convincing case for himself: Loyal, beyond all others! Overturner of pagan altars! Defender of the faith! But now he stood completely alone against the evil forces, and it was too much. He begged God to let him die and get off the scene. Elijah wanted out of what he was in. "Stop the world, God, I want off!"

Well, God did not stop the world, but God let Elijah off, and asked another man to get on. So it was that the mantle of Elijah fell on Elisha.

Now, Elisha was a man who in the same desperate time, with the same threatening woman on the premises, the same minority support, came with a fresh faith in God. And, at last, he saw the wicked removed, Baal-worship wiped out, justice established, and the house of the Lord back in business again.

But Elijah's inner defense had crumbled. He abdicated responsibility, demanding that history be on his terms instead of God's.

And what about you? Have you been saying, "God, stop the world: I want off"? Maybe you have already gotten off, brushed the church and all moral and spiritual responsibility off your hands.

Isn't this a good time to get back on? God is calling you, even as he did to Elijah, to get on your feet and stand once again with the people of God!

45. GOD IS IN A LOT OF TROUBLE

AT THE NATIONAL ZOO IN WASHINGTON, D. C., A BARBARIAN APE rattled the wires of his cage, as he had done a few thousand times before. This time, however, there was one slight difference — something gave. The wires parted and the ape soon found he could make room to squeeze himself through to freedom. In no time at all the keepers, visitors, the whole zoo was in trouble.

Zoo personnel came running with all the paraphernalia for capturing a wild animal. The libertine beast defied his would-be captors by ascending to the rooftop of one of the buildings. Finally, a gun was leveled at him, the trigger pulled, and a hypodermic dart went straight to target. In a matter of seconds the ape was tranquilized, and the keepers reached him with their nets and returned him to his cage.

If you ever get to that zoo, you will probably notice that one ape is obsessed with shaking his prison. He once had a taste of freedom, and now is earnestly hoping for another escape.

A zoo in trouble all because of a rebel ape! But God too is in trouble, and for much the same reason: Rebellion! The process of creating this world was apparently no trouble at all for God. There is no evidence of any huffing and puffing to fit a world together. No effort to toss the moon to ride like a ghostly galleon in the night. No difficulty orbiting a profusion of suns. No trouble raising his baton to fill the earth with a chorus of sound. No fuss, no muss in any of the first five days of creation!

But, on that day when God stooped down and gathered up a handful of earth and shaped it into a man, *that* day God got into a lot of trouble, and he's still in it.

I watched a television commercial being made by the use of pup-

104

pets. These characters were handled by two young performers who were voice and will for their puppets. Now, suppose those oversized stockings with faces could have decided to launch out on their own. What chaos would have reigned if they could have chosen to discard the script. No likelihood of this, however, for they were puppets, not people.

But this is the very trouble that God is in. He created *people*, not puppets. People can spread their silly legs and have nothing to do with the script. They can launch out on their own, leaving God shaking his head and regretting that he ever made man at all.

Edna St. Vincent Millay, pondering God's fashioning of the human heart and then setting it free, reportedly said: "I can't understand why he bothered in the first place; and I don't see for a moment how anything much can come of it. But how I respect him for daring to try!"

God took the risk because he felt it was worth taking. He wanted us to value what he values. And it is really a tremendous compliment that he would take this risk of our loving what he loves and, in it all, never coerce us. He always waits our voluntary response to "do justice, and to love kindness, and to walk humbly" with him.

You see, God respects you so much that he will not interfere with your sulking disobedience, nor force upon you a destiny you do not want. He considers this rebellion your privilege.

But, if you ever decide you want things his way and voluntarily seek his purpose for your life, how gracious will be his welcome! And even now he is ready to throw all the legions of heaven to your rescue. All he is waiting for is your simple assent.

46. "BREAKFAST WAS SUCH FUN"

SHE WAS PROPELLING HER WHEELCHAIR DOWN THE LONG HOSPITAL corridor toward me. Although she was the victim of some crippling disease and no longer young, you knew at once that she was no ordinary woman.

She completely captivated me with a rare radiance seldom found even in the fortunate and the healthy. Fate may have flung her into this wheelchair, but she rode it like a queen in her royal coach.

Now, conversation is inescapable with a soul like this. I quickly learned that, beneath the body malfunction, she was bearing a deep and lonely sorrow — six brief weeks ago she had lost her husband of 65 years. In just a few words she made it clear to me that, unlike so many marriages, hers had not been diminished by the years into a tired friendship.

In expressing her sorrow to me she did it in an odd and wondrously beautiful way. She explained, "Now that he is gone, the hardest moment of the day is breakfast." Never shall I forget the way her voice and eyes punctuated the sentence, and the sentence itself will linger with me always. The punctuation I can't share with you. But the sentence, I will. "Breakfast," she said, "was always such fun."

I figured it out. They spent over 23,000 breakfasts together in their 65 years, and now, as she looked back from her wheelchair over her life, the segments which came crowding back with healing memory were all those breakfasts together.

"Breakfast was always such fun!" Give that a moment's thought, will you? A woman facing the sunset — sick, lonely, bereaved — but what does she do? She puts her finger on the resplendent moments of her past and they glorify her present hour.

This, I think, is the mission of yesterday's mountaintop experiences! Yes, it's true, breakfast is a very small segment in any day, but after all isn't life a matter of small installments of glory against large installments of dullness? Around-the-clock bliss is rarely the lot of any of us. But neither is around-the-clock woe our portion. The most of us have had those moments when we were led "beside the still waters," or laid down in some "green pasture," or enjoyed a breakfast that was fun, which, if we could but return to them, would refresh our souls.

The Psalmist may be indicting you with his words: "They forgot what [God] had done. . . ." Is there any tragedy like this, the grave, sad, unfortunate forgetting of what God has done? Could this be the root of our cynicism? Is this why we are so often tempted to write God off completely? Do we permit the drain of the days to obscure all the "breakfasts" that were fun?

Is there any "burning bush" back there in your life before which you once stood excited and barefoot? Was there any morning when there was "manna from heaven" which you gathered with glee? If you could step back a moment from decrying your present circumstances, might you not discover, lurking in some dim corner of your memory, the training beauty of a forgotten joy?

It is so easy for us to let the mishaps of life, the dead places, and the deserts through which we travel obscure these past glories bestowed upon us by God! How easy to have them like some prodigal go to the "far country" of the mind! Oh, you didn't intend it this way. Yesterday's shimmering glory just got pushed out of sight in the stress of getting on with today's demands. You forgot how easy it is to forget.

So, if you are in one of those arid times when you feel the cold shoulder of God and you have a mind to vote him out of office, look and behold the lightning flashes in the night. They come from the resplendent glory of a gift once bestowed upon you by God.

It is in this that the restoring of the soul happens, I think, in remembering the "breakfasts" that were such fun.

May God restore your soul with the touch of yesterday's forgotten glory!

47. "QUIET . . . DISTURBANCE GOING ON"

TWO INCONGRUOUS STREET SIGNS CONFRONTED ME. ONE WAS A permanent sign erected close to a hospital exhorting everybody: "Quiet! Please!" The other sign was temporary, placed ten feet away from the "Quiet" sign and advised passing motorists that men were at work. The "men at work" were attacking a section of pavement with pneumatic drills that created a pandemonium of noise not easy to duplicate. The plea for quiet could not have been more severely violated if the Music Man had marched all his seventy-six trombones about the hospital.

Reflecting on this incongruity, I realized there was an analogy here between the church and the world. The "quiet" sign is up at the church pleading for peace and tranquility, the right to rest and pray and ponder noble thoughts about God. But men are at work in our world making all manner of disturbance. And the noise of it comes in our windows from Moscow, Berlin, Peking, Viet Nam, Mississippi!

Now, we resent this appalling turmoil under our window. We pray to God it will soon go away. But the men keep putting their drills into useless old things and in a convulsion of noise rip them to shreds.

We are accustomed to thinking that God absents himself from chaos, but I think in this we have been mistaken. God *brings* chaos! Whether it is the noise of the drills from the jungles of Africa, the cane fields of Cuba, or the campus of a southern university, God is in the disturbance. I must say this because this is what the Bible says.

God presides over even the tumult. He writes the agenda for history, and one thing on that agenda is the removal of sin and the coming of righteousness. Like any good engineer, God must pluck up and destroy what is unsound before he can build what is sound. And this is always disturbing, whether it is the dentist drilling out the decayed area of the tooth to fill the cavity or laborers drilling a broken pavement to build a new highway.

That there is a giant revolution going on in our world, few will dispute. But I am contending that God is party to that revolution. He brings judgment on the evil ways of men. Our God is a disturber, a consuming fire, a relentless enemy of rotten structures, and no pulling down of the shades on our minds, or erecting of "Quiet" signs will make it otherwise.

This is something that ought to get our minds off the Dow Jones averages for a minute. God is the presider over all those events on page one of your morning newspaper. Don't you see that when we fail to do justly and love mercy and walk humbly with our God, he is then, in his own way, shaking the corrupt things in society beneath us. And he will use flood and fire, exile and war when his people will not use justice, repentance, and faith.

And this is what makes our indifference and inertia so dangerous today. When we refuse to place the iniquity of our time, or any exploitation of persons, on our conscience; when we keep coming to terms with an unjust status quo; when we refuse to bestir ourselves against the misery blazing in the human family — God will bestir himself, and when he does we will be witness to an appalling disturbance, as he shakes to pieces all the things which displease him.

There is no quiet for us within the framework of a sinful status quo. God will see to that.

48. PRESENCE FOR CHRISTMAS

THOSE MAGI OF THE CHRISTMAS STORY PROBABLY CAME FROM THE shores of the Caspian Sea. Mounted on their shaggy camels, saddle bags bulging, they crossed the Tigris and the Euphrates, traversed the scorching desert, followed along the Dead Sea, and at last moved down the windswept road to David's town. They were motivated in this long trek by a bright new star in the heavens — a portent, they believed, of the birth of a king.

At the journey's end they found, in the straw of a stable, nothing spectacular — just a baby, poorly attended, crying, sleeping as all babies do. These men opened their saddle bags, bestowed their gifts, which were only disdained by the child, and, so the story reads, then returned to their own country.

There was something in the reading again of this old tale that pushed a button and turned on Christmas for me. What have you in this epic but PRESENTS, that is the gold, the myrrh, and the frankincense? And, what you very quickly do not have is PRESENCE, that is the men removed themselves, took leave to their own land. PRESENTS! And PRESENCE!

Now, those two words sound very similar, but there is considerable difference between them. I am suggesting that in these two words is the issue of Christmas. So prominent each Christmas are the gifts! This explains the crowds milling about in the stores, and the tide of extra mail at the post office. There is no doubt about the gifts at Christmas!

Just a warning, though, lest you make the effort: You cannot substitute PRESENTS for PRESENCE and still end up with the real significance of the holy season. Christmas is, at the bottom, not gifts but a Divine Presence!

110

Do you remember the announcement of the birth of Jesus? "Behold, a young woman shall conceive and bear a son, and you shall call his name Immanuel." The old scribe is careful to explain to us that "Immanuel" means the PRESENCE of God with us!

This is the message that the Bible never stops reciting. It is God's long-playing record which begins in "the cool of the day," when God walks in the garden with Adam and Eve. It is symbolized in a cloud by day and a fire-pillar by night as a million Hebrews wander out of Egypt toward the Promised Land. It leaps off the lips of the Psalmist when he says, "I will fear no evil; for thou art with me." It is in the thunder of those words spoken through Joshua: "Be not frightened, neither be dismayed; for the Lord your God is with you wherever you go."

It turns up in the Prophets even if one takes a ship to Tarshish and is swallowed by a giant fish, or thrust into fiery ovens, or put in with wild beasts. It is there, poignantly assuring, in the upper room: "Let not your hearts be troubled . . . where I am you may be also." It shouts from the Mount of Ascension: "Lo, I am with you always, to the close of the age." Paul puts it on parchment and the people of Rome take heart, even as we do: "Nor anything else . . . will be able to separate us from the love of God in Christ Jesus our Lord." And, it's there in a final curtain call as the Revelation is about to end: "Behold, the dwelling of God is with men. He will dwell with them, and they shall be his people."

PRESENCE! The Divine Presence all the way from Genesis to Revelation, from January 1 to December 31!

This, then, is Christmas — not gifts, but the Divine Gift.

May God this tide impart to you the blessing of his presence.

111

Walter I. Fishbaugh . . . is the university chaplain at the State College of Iowa, in Cedar Falls. His previous pastorates include churches in Woodstown, New Jersey, and Slatington, Pennsylvania.

John P. Gates . . . is pastor of the First Baptist Church in Bethesda, Maryland, president of the Baptist Ministers' Conference of the District of Columbia Baptist Convention, and president of the Bethesda Civitan Club. A past president of the Bethesda Council of Churches, he is active in various committees of the Council of Churches, National Capital Area. He is also a trustee of Crozer Theological Seminary and of the Welfare of the Blind, Inc.

Gustav H. Schlauch . . . is a teacher by profession, having spent a number of years in public school work before completing his doctorate at the University of Washington. Since then, he has been engaged in college teaching, first at Spokane University, then as head of the sociology department at Whitworth College in Spokane. He is a past president of the Washington Baptist Convention and the American Baptist Men of Washington State.

Edwin H. Tuller . . . is the general secretary of the American Baptist Convention. He serves on the Central Committee of the World Council of Churches, the General Board of the National Council of Churches, and the Executive Committee of the Baptist World Alliance. He has also served as executive secretary of the Massachusetts Baptist Convention and as general secretary of the Connecticut Council of Churches.

49. EXCUSE THE PERSONAL REFERENCE

THERE IS AN UNWRITTEN LAW THAT SPEAKERS SHOULD AVOID MAKING personal references when they address the public. This restriction is somewhat akin to the one that cautions a host and hostess from inflicting home movies on their dinner guests. The idea, of course, is that other people don't want to hear about you all the time. It doesn't take a lot of imagination to understand the how and why of such rules. Few of us have been spared an occasional encounter with a talkative bore who is the absolute focus of his own universe and who never fails to center on the one subject about which he is an expert — himself. Granting all this — and we have no choice — it still must be said that public utterance and private conversation can become unbearably dull if we must limit ourselves only to what someone else has said or someone else has written or someone else has done — somewhere else or other. There is something forceful, refreshing, and compelling about conversation in the first person singular. All the dangers aside, I prefer it to the sort of pale report of a second- or third-hand rumor which passes for conversation today. It is pallid and pithy, drained of all vitality because we are obsessed with being at least once removed from everything we say.

The next time a speaker mouths the simpering apology, "I hope you will excuse the personal reference," someone should lodge a formal and vigorous protest. It's high time we heard from each other. It's time what we talked about had our own fingerprints on it. It's time we let our conversation ring with brazen, first-hand frankness. Perhaps it's time we Christians remind ourselves that we profess to follow the one who could, and did, often say "You have heard that it was said to the men of old . . . but I say to you!" Those who listened to this kind of unapologetic personal

114

reference gaped with open mouth "for he taught them as one who had authority, and not as their scribes."

Perhaps it is this crusade of mine for the respectability, and indeed the sheer necessity, of "personal reference" that makes me so partial to the story of the blind man whom our Lord healed on the Sabbath. The spectacle of the offended religious authorities buzzing around in a tizzy trying to explain away a startling miracle of divine deliverance is one of the most pathetic and shocking commentaries on human sin and disbelief. All the clever power of their well-honed minds was marshaled in a shameful effort to avoid the obvious, lest they should be forced to ponder his claims and power. Into this academic discussion, so filled with tragic and comic elements, strides the man who is the object of their frustrations, the unwitting source of their embarrassment — a human being who is seeing for the first time in his life, born blind and newly healed. And he has the sublime good sense to say in effect: "You fellows amaze me! I am not particularly interested in your picky theological subtleties or your dishonest and devious attempts at arranging the evidences to suit your prejudices. I am an expert on one thing. This I know: I was blind and now I see. And furthermore, gentlemen, you'll have a hard time convincing me it was an evil man who could do me such good!" This is a ringing witness that makes me want to jump up and pump his hand. Spoken in the very heart of his personal competency. Where he was sure! Where he was an expert! Imagine, if you will, how ridiculous it would have been if he had begun all this by saying, "I hope you will forgive the personal reference."

In our churches and in our participation in the common life of our work and economic endeavor, we are all too often tongue-tied

Walter I. Fishbaugh

and mealy-mouthed. We think we lack the qualifications and the endowments necessary for effective witness to our faith and to our Lord. R. E. Day has a line that I like to quote from his book, *The Borrowed Glow*, in which he makes this simple statement: "Life's greatest endowment is an adequate experience of Christ." If you have really found God in his Son, if your encounter with Christ is a source of life-transforming power, you have the one qualification necessary to be an effective witness — so long, that is, as you talk about and witness to what you really know. Your encounter with Jesus Christ doesn't make you infallible, but it certainly should make you authentic. You have something worth talking about, something vital to tell. Something, actually, which only you can tell, for I think no two of us find God in exactly the same way.

My plea is not that we become a bunch of chatty egomaniacs obsessed with our own private world of religious experience. Religion is never private. But it is always personal, and there is a world of difference between personal religion and private religion. Our faith is an intensely personal relationship that brings us to new birth within the family of God. From the time of this new birth we are never again alone — never again isolated — never again private — always in relationship. My plea is for men and women to exploit for the sake of God's kingdom and for the sake of our lost world the one area of life in which each of us is an authority — the area of the personal work of God's grace in each of our lives.

If you were blind and now you can see, don't apologize that perhaps you don't understand it. And, above all, don't apologize for bearing witness to it. For God's sake and for the world's sake, stand up and be counted!

50. WHEN PEOPLE
RUB YOU THE WRONG WAY

THROWN WITH THEM IN LIFE, YOU ARE NOT IMPRESSED WITH THEM OR
attracted to them; you prefer not to be associated with them?
They irritate you? Among these persons may be your boss, a fellow
employee, a neighbor, or even a member of your family. How can
we best approach the problem of improving our relationship with
those whom we do not like?

You may say to yourself, "Well, it is my duty to get along with
this person. I'll force myself to make the best of my relationship
with him. I really don't care for him but I will put up a good
front." This attitude, of course, is far better than to mistreat or
break off relations with those you dislike, but living with others
simply out of a sense of duty brings problems, and is not the real
answer. It creates tensions.

For if you say, "It is my duty, even my Christian duty, to be
nice to a person," but inwardly hate him or despise him, you are
putting on a mask, so to speak, in order to make him think you
do not feel as you do. In doing this, you widen the gap between
your public behavior and your inner feelings. You become a divided personality. Immediately tension is created between what
you want to appear to be like from the outside and what you
really feel on the inside. You may live with these tensions for
a time, but there is a limit beyond which you cannot go. Eventu-
ally resentment will out and you will "blow your top," as we say.
We might be able to hold in our feelings at the office, but we let
them out at home. The people who love us most then pay for our
inability to do our duty toward those who irritate us. Sometimes,
trying desperately to get along with members of our family, we become so irritated and upset that we take it out on a fellow employee, a neighbor, or someone outside the home. Being nice out

117

of a sense of duty is not enough, if we are to have harmony and enjoy living with others.

To get along well with people, we must learn to love them. The apostle Paul called this "the more excellent way." We need to develop the capacity to love people whom we do not like. Most of us have been told from childhood that we ought to love our neighbor, but if the feeling of love is not in us we cannot command ourselves to love. If it is not in our hearts, where can we develop warmth of understanding and the desire really to care about another?

Actually, if we are fortunate enough to possess some love toward others, it is because we have responded to some love shown to us by our parents or someone along the line as we grew up. Frankly, if we have not experienced love in our childhood, we are at a disadvantage; we have a real handicap to overcome. But let us remember that God, who is love, has given every man some capacity to respond to love. To begin loving a person we must somehow start looking at him with different eyes, to try to look at him with the eyes of God, so to speak, to imagine how God looks at him.

What made it possible for Jesus to love his enemies who persecuted him? It was his ability to look at them with the eyes of God. He saw them not as hateful, malicious enemies, but rather as persons created by his Father who had lost their way, who had fallen from what God had intended them to be. So the apostle Paul advises us in writing to the Roman church, as translated in the Phillips edition of the Bible: "Open your hearts to one another as Christ has opened His heart to you, and God will be glorified."

If you do not find love in your heart for certain people, begin with the faith that God has placed a great value on every human being, even this person whom you do not care for. Furthermore, see him as a struggling fellow human being. Try to identify yourself in some way with him; to imagine how he looks at life, seeking to discover what some of his problems might be. Endeavor to look at him in a more objective manner, in a new light. Shift your stance toward him, as it were, and begin caring what happens to him as a person. Be ready to forgive and overlook his faults. Perhaps there is something which he might not like about you, and with good reason. Who is perfect? Reexamine your approach to him. Begin to love him.

If you do this, he may sense a change in your attitude and be drawn toward you. As a result of your love, he may change for the good. On the other hand, it may well be that any gesture of kindness on your part will be rebuffed. He may respond negatively. If this happens, you cannot force yourself into the soul of another. But you will find that endeavoring to love him in this way will be the means of relieving your own inner tensions. You may find yourself more capable of rising above your own feelings of resentment, becoming a less divided person and more of a unit. Whether he responds to you or not, you will have been delivered from your own inner conflict. This delivery will be a victory in itself, for with your change of heart, your own anxieties will diminish.

And if, perchance, this person does respond to your new love for him, you will have started a circle of understanding and reconciliation which will bring peace and perhaps even joy in your relationship with him. In human existence we are never entirely free from the clash of personalities, but by faith in God who is love, and with a little imagination, our living together can be vastly improved. So, "open your hearts to one another as Christ has opened His heart to you," and that person who irritates you might one day be a friend, and prove to you to be a blessing.

51. CHARGE IT

DID YOU EVER BUY AN ARTICLE, CHARGE IT, AND THEN, WHEN YOU got home with it, ask yourself why you bought it? As the teen-age heroine of the comic strip "Penny" once said, "It's funny how cheap everything seems when you charge it, and how revoltingly expensive it is when you come to pay for it."

Let us examine three aspects of this business of charging, whether we charge to ourselves or to someone else.

First, we sometimes charge things to others, without even intending to do so. How about the man who has had a hard time at the office, and comes home out of sorts, then vents his ill temper on his wife, or the children, or even the dog or cat? There is also the individual who goes to church or to some other public meeting and whispers constantly to his seat-mate, not thinking at all about the other people, who have come to worship, or at least to listen. I remember one funeral I attended, where just in front of me sat two women who disrespectfully whispered and gestured during the whole service.

A second idea about charging to others has to do with blaming someone else for our own mistakes or shortcomings. We have a number of examples of this in the Bible. When Adam and Eve had eaten the forbidden fruit in the Garden of Eden, Adam blamed Eve, and Eve blamed the serpent. When Aaron made the golden calf while Moses was on Mount Sinai, and Moses on his return took him to task for it, Aaron put the blame on the children of Israel. He did not have the courage to accept the responsibility for his own acts as leader of the people.

We often do this kind of charging. On the college campus we often hear such excuses as these: "It was the room-mate I had," "It was the crowd I ran with," "The boys in my dorm." After he

120

Gustav H. Schlauch

is married, the man may blame his wife, as did Adam: "The woman whom thou gavest to be with me."

A more serious aspect of this charging to someone else is charging to the person we are going to be. Let us look at Willie Brown, in the seventh grade. He will soon be Bill Brown in high school or college; then, just a few years later, Mr. William K. Brown in the occupational world. Willie wastes his time in school, not learning to read effectively, unable to follow through on his assignments. As a result, when he is Bill, he fails to win the scholarship to college or graduate school. He may be so poorly prepared that he even fails to graduate from college. More serious even than this, it may be some defect in character that Willie or Bill has developed, little realizing how he was undermining the possible career of the person he was going to be. Willie was charging costly items to Bill, and Bill in his turn to William K., which they would have great difficulty in paying, if indeed they could pay them at all. An example on the positive side comes from the life of Daniel Webster, who won an important historic case in court, known as the Dartmouth College Case, with the information he had compiled while working on what seemed at the time an insignificant case, hardly worth the effort of looking up all that data. But if Webster had slighted this preparation, he would have charged something very costly against his own future.

A third aspect of charging items is that there is always a reckoning day. Once we had a little neighbor girl who went to the neighborhood store with some little friends of hers, and came home with a rather large bag of candy. Her mother, knowing that she had taken no money with her, asked her where she got the candy. She replied, "Oh, I charged it. The other girls were charg-

Gustav H. Schlauch

ing things, so I thought I would too." Her mother asked her who was going to pay for it, and she replied, "I didn't know it had to be paid for. I thought when you charged it that was all."

We laugh at such simplicity, but many of us go ahead blithely, in many of life's relationships, acting as if the bill did not ever have to be paid. We push along selfishly, then wake up to find that we have no friends. We play fast and loose with character traits, then find that people have lost confidence in us, and that we cannot even face our own reflection in the mirror. We follow the line of least resistance, then find that we have not developed the skills, the stamina, the understanding, to accomplish what we most desire. We charge things to others and to the person that we later become, and find it exceedingly difficult or even impossible to pay what has been charged.

There is some hope, however. There is someone to whom we can charge anything. One prayer recorded in the New Testament has made a deep impression on me, the one prayed by Christ on the Cross: "Father, forgive them; for they know not what they do." Christ was really saying, "Father, charge this to me." And he had a right to ask that, for he had, and has, unlimited credit with his Father, God, so that his requests will be honored. He can charge anything to himself; he stands good for all *your* debts.

But there is a price you must pay if you avail yourself of this unlimited credit. You must accept him, and give him the chief place in your heart and your life. This is dangerous, for he will change your whole way of living. He will give you a new spirit. He will change your very nature. This is why we say, "Christ is the answer." Why don't you dedicate your life to him today?

52. FAITH FOR A TROUBLED TIME

THE WORLD IS IN TURMOIL. DISCORD AND UNREST SEEM ALL ABOUT us. Does your faith help you to face life with assurance? It can, if you have an adequate faith.

Jesus preached in a time of great unrest to a people who felt the stigma and sting of a tyrannical power. To them he said, "Come to me, all who labor and are heavy-laden, and I will give you rest."

What did he mean by that?

Near the outbreak of the Korean War, I was invited to take part in a religious emphasis week at my college alma mater. Of particular interest to me was the theme that the young people had chosen for discussion: "A Steady Mind in an Unsteady World." I was assigned a discussion group on this theme and began something as follows:

"I am very much interested in the theme you have chosen for your discussion, 'A Steady Mind in an Unsteady World,' but I propose that we forget the first part for a moment and get down to the second part, 'an Unsteady World.' What is so unsteady about the world in which we live?"

They replied, "You're kidding!" But I said, "No; I'm serious. Just what is so unsteady about our world today?" So they went on and poured out for me a story I knew all too well — the story of a student generation in the midst of war. When they had finished, I simply said this: "When I was a student in the halls of this very same university, we were in the midst of an economic depression. We had no money to pay our bills. There were no jobs. Men with children hungry at

Edwin H. Tuller

home were walking the streets in search of employment. Students regularly ate beans and macaroni, macaroni and beans — anything to fill up hungry stomachs. And after four years of struggle to keep body and soul together, we got our prized sheepskin, marched triumphantly down College Hill to the marketplaces only to discover to our dismay that no one was looking for our services, college degree or no college degree. If we could find a job anywhere — at the bottom of the ladder or below — we counted ourselves lucky and took it in stride.

"Now," I continued, "I recite this to you young people today not to seek for your sympathy. We of our generation don't need that. But simply to suggest that if you are waiting for the time in this life when everything is made to your liking, you have a long wait ahead of you. I am not a pessimist, but I have been in the Christian ministry long enough to know that even if there is no war or economic depression, personal tragedy can strike without warning at any time. My own Dad was killed instantly in an automobile accident when I was a senior in college. The question is: When the world in which you live suddenly becomes unsteady, what do you have to uphold you?

"Let's get down to business," I continued, "and discuss something that really matters: your faith. Is it a faith adequate for any tragedy you might be called upon to bear? The Psalmist speaks to this need when he writes, 'God is our refuge and strength, a very present help in trouble. Therefore we will not fear though the earth should change, though the mountains shake in the heart of the sea; though its waters roar and foam,

though the mountains tremble with its tumult. . . . Be still,
and know that I am God. I am exalted among the nations, I
am exalted in the earth! The Lord of Hosts is with us; the
God of Jacob is our refuge.' Did he mean what he said?"

Some years ago I stood in the ancient and ruined city of Pompeii.
To my left there towered smoking Mt. Vesuvius, still throwing its
ash from its bed of molten lava. To my right were the peaceful
waters of the blue Mediterranean, lapping lazily at the foothills
beneath. My mind went back in history to the time when all about
me was a thriving city. One day the people looked up to see the
molten lava come down the side of the mountain ever closer to
their village. They knew that they would have to run for their
lives. So they jumped into their little boats and set out to sea, only
to have a tidal wave dash them back against the shore.

Now, had I been there in that day, could I have said with the
Psalmist, "God is our refuge and strength, a very present help in
trouble. Therefore we will not fear though the earth should change,
though the mountains shake in the heart of the sea; though its
waters roar and foam, though the mountains tremble with its
tumult"?

Did he mean *that?* He said it; and I for one believe he meant it.
What he said, and Jesus after him, is that there is nothing in this
world, in life, or in death that has the power to separate men of
faith from God. God alone is a sure refuge in time of trouble.

I invite you today to come to Jesus Christ, all ye that labor and
are heavy laden with trouble, and find rest unto your souls. Make
his faith yours — a faith for troubled times.

TOPICAL INDEX